# THE BOOK OF WISDOM

## VOLUME 1 AND 2

The Hidden Order Behind All Things

The Hidden Architecture

**Copyright © 2025 The Hidden Architecture**
All rights reserved.

ISBN: 979-8-89860-327-4

No part of this publication may be reproduced, stored in a retrieval system, or transmitted in any form or by any means—electronic, mechanical, photocopying, recording, or otherwise—without the prior written permission of the author or publisher. All rights reserved under international and Pan-American copyright conventions.

**Legal Notice:** This publication is intended for personal use only. You may not modify, distribute, sell, use, quote, or paraphrase any part of this book without explicit consent from the author or publisher.

**Disclaimer:** The information contained within this book is provided for educational and entertainment purposes only. The author and publisher have made every effort to ensure the accuracy and completeness of the information presented. However, no warranties of any kind are expressed or implied. This book does not constitute legal, financial, medical, or professional advice. Readers should consult qualified professionals before applying any of the information contained herein. By reading this book, the reader agrees that the author and publisher shall not be held liable for any damages, losses, or liabilities caused directly or indirectly by the use or misuse of the information contained in this book, including but not limited to errors, omissions, or inaccuracies.

*This is not for everyone. And yet it belongs to all.*

## Table of Contents

**VOLUME I** .................................................................................. 7

    Introduction .......................................................................... 8

    Chapter I: The Silent Law Before All Things ............................ 22

    Chapter II: The Chamber of the Double Flame ....................... 31

    Chapter III: The Path of the Serpent and the Staff ................. 41

    Chapter IV: The Hidden Geometry of the Soul ....................... 50

    Chapter V: The Waters That Remember ................................ 62

    Chapter VI: The Guardian of the Threshold ........................... 72

    Chapter VII: The Seed That Contains the Star ....................... 82

**VOLUME II** ............................................................................. 94

    Introduction ........................................................................ 95

    Chapter VIII: The Circle That Has No End ............................ 107

    Chapter IX: The Tongue That Speaks Without Sound .......... 118

    Chapter X: The Breath Between Two Worlds ....................... 130

    Chapter XI: The Fire That Does Not Burn ............................ 141

    Chapter XII: The Veil of the Infinite Faces ............................ 150

    Chapter XIII: The Throne in the Cave of the Heart ............... 159

    Chapter XIV: The Word That Was Never Written ................. 175

# VOLUME I

# The Veil and the Awakening

# Introduction

*There is a silence that lives beneath the noise of the world. A subtle vibration that calls to those who have begun to see through the shimmer of surface living. You may not know when it began. Perhaps it was in a moment of stillness, when something ancient stirred in your chest. Perhaps it was during a season of unraveling, when the truths you'd once clung to crumbled beneath your feet. Or perhaps it's been with you always — a quiet ache behind the eyes, a sense that this life, in its common rhythms, is only a fragment of something far greater.*

---

This part of the journey begins here — in the territory between forgetting and remembrance.

The modern world offers countless answers, but very little wisdom. We are surrounded by a million names for things, yet disconnected from the essence behind them. Spirituality has been carved into trends, knowledge flattened into data, and truth diluted into a stream of performances. And yet, underneath the digital static and the culturally conditioned self, the old path still exists — the one walked in silence, in vision, in fire and shadow, by those who came before and those who dared to remember.

*The Book of Wisdom* does not aim to teach you something new. It is here to uncover what you already know. What was buried. What was sealed behind layers of language, belief, fear, and distraction. This volume begins the work of peeling back those layers — not to give you more ideas to carry, but to offer a return to the place inside you that remembers what is sacred.

The veil is not out there. It is within. It is the accumulation of everything you've been told you must be in order to be safe, acceptable, successful, enlightened. It is the distortion between your original nature and your performed identity. To awaken is not to acquire, but to remove — to burn the masks with the flame of presence, until only the essential remains.

Each chapter in this volume is a threshold. Some will feel like recognition. Others may provoke, disorient, or press against the edges of your current understanding. That is by design. Initiation has never been about comfort.

It is about re-alignment with truth — and truth has never bowed to our preferences.

You will not find quick answers here. What you will find are keys — some wrapped in symbol, others in silence. You will encounter teachings that do not seek to convince, but to **activate**. Every word is chosen not to inform, but to awaken the part of you that already knows, already sees, already remembers.

This is not a doctrine. It is not a system of belief. It is not meant to be followed. It is meant to be entered.

There is no dogma here. Only thresholds. Only echoes. Only invitations to listen differently.

You are not being asked to agree with anything. You are being asked to feel what resonates not with your mind, but with the deeper current that runs through your spine, your dreams, your breath. That which knows what cannot be proven.

This part of the book is called *The Veil and the Awakening* because these are the twin movements that begin the journey. The unveiling of illusion. The return of perception. What was fragmented must be seen as whole. What was asleep must rise. What was once hidden in mystery must be encountered in stillness.

Do not rush. Do not skim. This is not a race. It is a ritual.

Let the words touch you. Let the symbols pass through your skin. Let the old parts of you dissolve, not with struggle, but with reverence.

You are not here to master this wisdom.

You are here to remember that it has always been yours.

# The Noise That Conceals the Signal

*In every era, wisdom has had to contend with interference. But never before has the interference been so constant, so invasive, and so brilliantly disguised as importance.*

---

The modern seeker is not surrounded by silence, as initiates once were in temples and caves. Instead, they are enveloped in a thick and endless noise — a stream of updates, opinions, images, headlines, and surface-level solutions. This noise does not come only from the outside. Over time, it seeps inward and begins to speak with the voice of the self.
You may feel it as the constant pull toward urgency. As the tension in your chest when you wake up and reach for your device before your breath has fully landed in your body. You may feel it in the quiet moments, too, when the thought of being still becomes strangely uncomfortable, even frightening. This is not simply distraction. It is fragmentation. And fragmentation is the enemy of wisdom.
Noise is not just sound. It is anything that pulls your awareness away from its natural stillness. It is anything that replaces presence with performance, reflection with reaction, truth with trend. It floods the senses and narrows the field of attention, making the sacred seem irrelevant and the trivial seem urgent.
In such an environment, the signal — the subtle pulse of truth, of knowing, of deep intuition — is not destroyed. It is concealed. It becomes harder to locate, not because it is lost, but because the inner ear has forgotten how to recognize it.
The spiritual path does not begin with learning more. It begins with unlearning the noise. Before you can remember what is essential, you must begin to notice what is artificial. You must become attuned to the distortions that have shaped your perception, to the ways you've internalized the volume of the world as your own voice.
Most people do not even realize they are in a trance. Not a mystical trance, but a cultural one. A trance of immediacy, consumption, competition. This trance tells you to be more, have more, know more, share more, and do it all quickly. It rewards speed over clarity, novelty over wisdom, visibility over depth. The more noise you absorb, the more it begins to form your internal

world — until the soul's signal becomes a whisper buried beneath layers of stimulation and urgency.

But the signal is still there.

It never leaves. Even when buried beneath years of noise, the signal continues pulsing. It waits patiently beneath your strategies, beneath your fears, beneath your identities. It is quieter than the noise, not because it is weaker, but because it does not force itself. Truth never shouts. It waits to be heard.

You may have felt it as a strange dissonance while scrolling through a sea of advice, teachings, or inspiration. That subtle tug inside that says, *Something here is off. This isn't it.* You may not have known how to name it, but you felt it. That tension between saturation and starvation — between the appearance of wisdom and the absence of real nourishment.

This book is not here to add more noise to your life. It is here to create the conditions in which the signal can become audible again. But for that to happen, you must begin to notice the noise. Not resist it, not fight it, but *notice* it. Awareness is the first step. Noticing how often you are pulled out of your body. How often your thoughts are not your own. How often silence feels unbearable.

This noticing is not passive. It is the beginning of reclamation. Once you see the noise for what it is — once you feel how it vibrates differently than truth — you begin to reclaim the ground of your awareness. You begin to remember what it feels like to be present without performing.

*You begin to hear again.*

The more you listen to what lies beneath the noise, the more you begin to recognize its texture. It does not demand your attention. It does not beg to be heard. It does not come wrapped in validation or excitement. It moves like breath through still water. It does not sell you anything. It does not flatter you. It simply reveals. And what it reveals is not always comfortable, but it is always real.

To listen in this way requires a kind of inner quiet that is not just the absence of sound, but the absence of scrambling. It is the stillness that remains when you no longer chase meaning outside of yourself. It is not about retreating from the world, but about entering the world differently — from a center that is anchored in the real, not the reactive.

In ancient temples, before initiates were given access to sacred knowledge, they were taught to empty. Not just physically, but mentally, emotionally, energetically. They were stripped of attachments, beliefs, and illusions. Not as punishment, but as preparation. Because truth, when it arrives, requires space. It cannot enter where there is no room.

In our time, we have reversed the order. We try to fill ourselves first, hoping that truth will land on top of the accumulation. But truth has never worked that way. It is not layered onto chaos. It rises from clarity. The wisdom you are seeking is not something external that you must acquire, but something internal that you must *make room for*.

There is no single method to silence the noise, but there is a way to become so deeply attuned to the signal that the noise loses its grip. This is not a discipline of avoidance, but of refinement. It means choosing slowness when everything urges you to speed up. It means valuing depth when everything is designed to skim. It means remembering that not all input is nourishment.

There is a power in reclaiming the right to be unavailable to the noise. Not in arrogance, but in reverence. You are not here to consume everything. You are not meant to be a receiver of every current, every opinion, every frequency that floods the collective field. The soul is not a storage device. It is a vessel of discernment.

This discernment is not about judgment, but about resonance. When you encounter truth, even in a single sentence, it stirs something deep within you. A signal that moves not in your logic, but in your marrow. You feel it before you understand it. You know it before you can explain it. It does not flatter the ego. It humbles and strengthens all at once. That is the signal.

You are being asked to remember how to recognize it.

There will still be noise. The world will not quiet itself for your awakening. But you can cultivate a different relationship to it. You can begin to hear the difference between static and signal. You can stop treating noise as a source of identity. You can stop confusing volume with value. And in doing so, you will begin to realign your internal compass.

Wisdom is not louder than the world. It is just clearer. And the more you align with it, the more the rest fades into the background. The more you walk in its rhythm, the more you realize you are not here to fight the noise — you are here to become immune to it.

This subchapter is not a solution. It is a beginning. A tuning of the ear. A refinement of perception. A shift from consumption to presence.

There is a signal inside you that is older than language and deeper than fear. You do not need to create it. You only need to stop mistaking the static for truth.

From this moment forward, your task is not to find more. It is to hear more clearly. And to hear more clearly, you must be willing to become still. Even when the world insists that stillness is wasted time. Even when every conditioned part of you resists it.

Because in that stillness, something begins to stir. Not another idea. Not another answer. But something infinitely more valuable.

You.

The signal is not separate from you. It is you — when all else falls away.

## The Fragrance of the Forgotten Path

*There are moments in life when something ancient brushes past you — not with force, but with the softness of a scent carried by the wind. You cannot trace where it came from. You cannot explain it. But in its presence, something in your chest stirs. The world quiets for just an instant, and a memory without image, a knowing without form, begins to rise. This is the beginning of the return.*

---

The forgotten path is not forgotten because it was erased. It was buried — under repetition, fear, conquest, and noise. It was covered by systems that had no use for the sacred. It was made invisible by the logic of empires, reduced to metaphor or myth. But the path itself never disappeared. It remains where it has always been: in the marrow, in the dreams, in the breath between thoughts.

You have walked this path before. Not in the same body. Not in the same language. But the movement is familiar. It calls to the part of you that knows the turning of seasons in the dark, that understands the language of silence, that bows before symbols it cannot fully translate. The path is not ahead of you. It is beneath your feet, waiting for you to recognize it.

When something is forgotten, it is not destroyed. It waits. And often, it reveals itself in strange ways — through discomfort, through longing, through the persistent sense that there is something more, something deeper, just beyond the edges of your current understanding. This longing is not a flaw. It is guidance. It is the intelligence of the soul reminding you that you did not come here to adapt. You came here to remember.

Remembering does not happen all at once. It is not an idea you can grasp or a fact you can recite. It unfolds like fragrance — subtle, nonlinear, impossible to measure. You do not remember the path through effort. You remember it through resonance. Through moments of alignment where something inside you says, *Yes. This is true. I've known this before.*

In these moments, the body often responds before the mind does. Your breath changes. Your skin tingles. Time stretches. You feel the presence of something more real than reality as it has been defined for you. You are not learning. You are being returned to.

This return often begins in solitude. Not loneliness, but sacred solitude — the kind that reveals how much of your life has been shaped by forgetting. You begin to notice the ways you've been taught to abandon your inner knowing, to trade intuition for approval, to silence what was inconvenient to the world around you. You begin to feel the cost of that forgetting. And in that awareness, the path becomes visible again.

But seeing the path and walking it are not the same.

To walk the path is to choose it again and again, even when it is not convenient, even when no one else sees it, even when it threatens the roles you've learned to play. It is not a straight line. It moves in spirals, through descent and ascent, through fire and rest. It asks for your presence, not your perfection.

The fragrance may arrive in unexpected places — in a phrase from a stranger, in the quiet after grief, in the awe of looking at a sky too vast to explain. It is not logical. It does not follow the patterns you've been trained to trust. But it is trustworthy. And the more you follow it, the more the path reveals itself. Not as a destination, but as a way of being.

You may begin to notice how little the world honors this path. You will not find signs pointing to it in the usual places. There are no rewards offered for remembering. No applause for tuning in to the unseen. In fact, much of what you recall may seem to place you at odds with what others call reality. That, too, is part of the initiation.

The ancient ones spoke often in paradox and symbol because they knew that the deepest truths were not meant to be argued. They were meant to be lived. The more you try to explain what you are remembering, the more it may seem to dissolve under the pressure of language. That is not failure. That is proof that what you're touching belongs to a realm deeper than intellect.

You are not meant to explain the fragrance. You are meant to follow it.

And yet, even as you follow, you may find yourself doubting. You may ask: *Is this real, or am I just imagining it?* You may feel foolish for trusting something so intangible. But this, too, is part of what has been unlearned. In a world obsessed with certainty, we've forgotten how to follow feeling. We've abandoned the intelligence that moves through subtlety. And so, to return to this way of knowing will feel unfamiliar — not because it is new, but because it is ancient.

Do not expect the forgotten path to feel clear at every step. It is not a straight road paved with signs. It is a living current. A movement that requires your full presence. Often, you will not know where it leads until you have already arrived. And even then, it may not look the way you imagined. It may strip you before it blesses you. It may dismantle your certainty before it gives you peace.

There will be moments when it asks you to let go of what you once believed was necessary. The path will not always be comfortable, but it will always be exact. It will lead you into the landscapes of your own soul — the ones you've hidden from, the ones you've longed to find, the ones you didn't know existed. It will take you to the edges of yourself, not to break you, but to show you that you were never only what you thought.

This is not about transcending the world. It is about walking through it differently. With reverence. With attunement. With the quiet confidence that comes from having remembered your original orientation — not toward success, not toward approval, but toward alignment.

The fragrance is what brings you back to that orientation. It is the subtle thread that pulls you inward when the outer world feels too loud. It is the invisible guide that reminds you to listen differently, to walk slower, to see symbol where others see nothing. And the more you follow it, the more your inner landscape begins to change. Your senses sharpen. Your dreams deepen. Your intuition begins to speak again — not in riddles, but in resonance.

You do not need to rush this return. Nothing essential is in danger of being lost. The path waits for you. It always has. Even when you wandered, even when you forgot, it did not close. You were never cast out. You simply turned your gaze elsewhere.

But now, something is stirring. Not as a demand, but as a remembrance. And if you have felt the faint scent of something ancient returning to your awareness, you are already on the path. You do not need to believe it. You only need to continue. The knowing will unfold as you walk.

There is no final destination. There is only deeper recognition.

The forgotten path is not hidden from you. It is hidden *by* you — covered by years of inherited noise and layers of false identities. But its fragrance still rises through the cracks. And now, you are beginning to notice. You are

beginning to trust it again. You are beginning to remember not just what the path is, but who you are when you walk it.
And that changes everything.

**When the Soul Whispers Through the Cracks**

*There are places in life where things break.*

---

Not catastrophically, not with the drama of disaster, but quietly, like the slow splitting of something once held too tightly together. A relationship frays. A certainty dissolves. A chapter closes without your consent. The ground beneath your identity begins to tremble, not enough to collapse it completely, but just enough to reveal the hollowness in its foundation.
These are the cracks.
They are not accidents. They are invitations.
Most people try to patch them as quickly as possible. They reach for distractions, explanations, solutions. Anything to fill the empty space that has suddenly opened up. But there is a moment, just before the instinct to fix arises, where something else tries to come through. Something softer. Something older. It does not demand. It does not explain. It does not promise anything. It simply whispers.
That whisper is the soul.
It does not speak in full sentences. It does not hand you a plan. It does not argue with your confusion. It comes in images, sensations, phrases that land in your body like echoes from a place you had forgotten existed. And it never forces itself. If you are too quick to patch the crack, you may miss it. But if you pause — if you are still enough to feel — you will notice that what emerges from the fracture is not failure, but light.
The soul does not speak in the language of the surface. It speaks from underneath. Beneath the roles, beneath the narratives, beneath the stories you have been told and the stories you have told yourself. It lives in the places that have not been domesticated by culture or numbed by repetition. And because of this, it often has no choice but to speak through disruption. When life is too full, the soul becomes inaudible. It needs space. It needs silence. And most often, it finds that space in the very places you would least choose — the unravelings, the losses, the emptiness that stretches without end.
You may have felt this already. In the middle of grief, when everything else fell away and something pure rose up inside of you — not joy, not clarity,

but a kind of knowing that didn't come from the mind. Or during moments of uncertainty, when the idea of who you thought you were began to slip, and what remained was strangely still, strangely familiar. That presence is the soul. Not a fantasy, not a concept, but the deepest part of you trying to return to the surface of your life.

It does not need to be awakened. It is already awake. What it needs is your attention.

The soul does not chase. It does not compete with the noise. It waits. And when a crack opens, it steps forward. Not to take over, but to be met. The meeting does not require perfection. It requires honesty. You do not need to be whole to hear the soul. You only need to be open. The soul is not afraid of your fragmentation. It does not ask you to be clean before you come to it. In fact, it often prefers the moments when your surface begins to crumble. Because that is when the light can get in. That is when your true self begins to reassemble, not according to old patterns, but according to a deeper rhythm.

You cannot chase the whisper, but you can learn how to meet it. Not by striving, but by softening. By allowing what breaks in you to stay open a little longer before the instinct to rebuild takes over. Most have been taught that cracks must be healed quickly, that discomfort must be resolved, that emptiness is a sign of something gone wrong. But the soul lives in these spaces. It uses them. It slips between the edges of what is no longer working and plants the seeds of what might become.

This is why collapse, when faced with awareness, often becomes the birthplace of vision. Not the kind of vision you can explain or map out, but the kind that shifts the atmosphere of your being. You begin to see your life not only as a timeline of events, but as a conversation with something deeper. You begin to understand that the hard seasons, the ruptures, the dissolving structures, were not just accidents or punishments. They were the soul's architecture, shaking loose everything that was built without it.

There is wisdom in not rushing to repair. There is power in letting the pieces lie where they fall, even if only for a moment, so that you can feel what has been hiding underneath. When the masks drop, when the noise dulls, when the scaffolding of identity begins to loosen, you are not left with nothing. You are left with what was always true. That quiet presence that does not perform. That subtle hum of awareness that needs no stage. That is the voice behind the whisper.

To live in alignment with the soul does not mean you no longer feel pain or confusion. It means you stop seeing those things as obstacles. You begin to recognize them as doors. The grief you carry, the longing that doesn't fade, the tension that doesn't resolve — these are not flaws to be eliminated. They are signals. They are entry points. And the soul speaks through them because it knows that truth rarely enters through certainty. It enters through surrender.

There may come a time when you stop fearing the cracks. Not because they stop hurting, but because you learn to see what comes through them. You begin to trust that every rupture carries a message, and every silence has something to reveal. You stop expecting the soul to speak in moments of clarity and start listening in the spaces where you feel most undone.

And that is where the real conversation begins.

The soul does not want you to escape the world. It wants you to return to it differently. To walk with an awareness that does not need to dominate or explain. To create, speak, move, and relate from a place that is rooted in what is real. Not what is marketed as truth. Not what is celebrated as enlightenment. But what is ancient and trembling and luminous beneath it all.

If you are still waiting for the voice of the soul to arrive like thunder, you may miss the way it already speaks through the rustle of leaves, through the ache in your chest when something sacred stirs, through the quiet after disappointment, through the dream that lingers after waking. The whisper is already here. It always was.

And now, as you learn to listen, not with your ears, but with your entire being, you begin to realize that the cracks are not flaws. They are thresholds. The soul never needed perfection to speak. It only needed an opening.

And now that you've heard it — however faint, however fleeting — you cannot unhear it.

The conversation has begun.

This is not a book of conclusions, but of initiations.
Each chapter begins not with explanation, but with an opening — a threshold.
Let the rhythm guide you. Let the echoes deepen. What repeats is not repetition. It is remembering.

# Chapter I: The Silent Law Before All Things

## The Word Before Sound

*Long before language was carved into the air, before breath gave shape to vibration and meaning, there was a silence that held everything. Not an absence, but a fullness. A presence beyond articulation. This was the original Word — not spoken, not written, but inherent. The Word before sound is not a concept. It is the undivided potential from which all form arises. It is not what you hear, but what makes hearing possible.*

---

Many traditions speak of a primordial sound — a sacred syllable, a cosmic vibration, a divine utterance that brought the world into being. But even before that vibration moved, there was an impulse. A silent knowing. A wordless awareness. This is the seed-state of wisdom. It is not yet expression. It is origin. It is what every truth is trying to return to.

Modern minds are trained to look for answers in articulation. We want things to be explained, defined, made digestible. But true wisdom often refuses to enter the world of easy language. It resists reduction. It speaks best in silence, in symbol, in states of being that cannot be translated without distortion. And so, the Word before sound remains hidden — not because it is far, but because it is too close. Too native to the soul for the mind to claim as its own.

You may have felt this Word in moments where nothing needed to be said, and yet everything was understood. When standing before something so vast, so raw, that language would have only diminished it. Or in the presence of another, where the space between you held more truth than any sentence could convey. These are not moments of absence. They are moments of return. The Word before sound lives in them — not as information, but as direct knowing.

This kind of knowing cannot be taught. It can only be reawakened. And reawakening begins with a kind of reverent unlearning. It requires you to soften your grip on explanation. To become quiet enough inside to notice what pulses beneath the noise of interpretation. It asks you to trust a deeper layer of recognition — the kind that does not arrive through thought, but through stillness.

Before sound became a tool for naming and controlling, it was an expression of harmony. The first sounds were echoes of the unspoken. Their purpose was not to define the world, but to align with it. They arose not from intellect, but from presence. Chant, breath, tone — these were not techniques, they were transmissions. They carried the frequency of the original Word, still vibrating beneath all things.

We have not lost this connection. We have only forgotten how to attune to it. Because the modern world treats silence as emptiness, stillness as unproductive, and ambiguity as weakness. But the Word before sound cannot be grasped by a restless mind. It requires a different kind of listening. A listening that does not reach outward, but folds inward. Not toward more content, but toward a finer quality of contact.

To carry the Word before sound is not to recite, but to radiate. It is to embody a vibration that has not been broken into syllables, a clarity that precedes the division of thought. You do not need to speak to share it. In fact, its presence is most powerful when no words are used at all. It moves through you like scent through a room, altering the atmosphere without declaring itself.

Somewhere within you, this Word still lives. Not as an idea, but as your original coherence. It is the alignment beneath your voice, the still point beneath your movement. And even when your speech is tangled, when your expressions fall short, the Word remains intact. It is not harmed by your forgetting. It waits.

You begin to embody it when you stop performing. When you allow silence to stretch without rushing to fill it. When your presence becomes more rooted than your opinions. When your being speaks more than your language. In those moments, others may not know what you are doing, but they will feel something settle in themselves just by being near you. This is not charisma. It is resonance.

Resonance is not created. It is uncovered. And what it resonates with is that silent, sacred source that breathes beneath all form. It has no agenda, no argument. It is not here to convince. It is here to remind. And when you align with it, you begin to speak differently. Not louder. Not with more authority. But with a kind of clarity that cuts through noise without raising its voice.

There are teachers who carry this. You may have met them, even in passing. Their words do not shimmer with polish. Their gestures are often simple. But when they speak, something inside you listens more deeply than usual. Not because of what is said, but because of what stands behind it. They are not trying to sound wise. They are aligned with the Word that lives behind wisdom.

This alignment cannot be faked. It cannot be rehearsed. The Word before sound is not a technique. It is a state. And it reveals itself only when the surface noise is quieted long enough for truth to rise without force. You cannot bend it to your will. You can only empty yourself of what it is not. Of mimicry. Of grasping. Of cleverness. And then, in that open space, something begins to speak through you.

Not every silence leads to this. Some silences are just the absence of noise. But the silence that precedes the Word is alive. It does not feel empty. It feels dense, luminous, intimate. When you are in it, you know. Not because you understand, but because you recognize. Something ancient in you responds, not with thoughts, but with stillness.

That is the space from which all sacred speech is born. That is the soil in which real language is grown. And when you speak from that soil, your words may be few, but they carry weight. They don't need to explain. They don't need to convince. They echo in the space between people, and something within the listener begins to stir.

You do not need to strive for this. You only need to become available. The Word is already within you. Not as a destination to be reached, but as a root to return to. Every time you listen more than you react, pause more than you project, feel more than you perform, you move closer to it. Not to possess it, but to remember that it is the quiet core of who you are.

Let that remembering continue. Let it shape your expression, not by giving you the right things to say, but by anchoring your voice in something deeper than language. The Word before sound is not a thing to speak. It is a way to live.

# The Pulse of Formless Order

*There is an order that existed long before structure. An intelligence that shaped stars, carved rivers, and choreographed the unfolding of galaxies without blueprints, without commands, without control. It is not the order of rules or grids, but of rhythm. It moves like breath through the vastness of the unseen. It governs not by decree, but by alignment. It does not impose. It reveals. And its movement is a pulse — slow, steady, invisible, yet unmistakably alive.*

---

We live in a world addicted to structure. To outlines, systems, and step-by-step processes. There is safety in the visible frame. We are taught to seek clarity through definitions, control through categorization. But the soul does not belong to that kind of order. It does not move in straight lines. It does not develop according to fixed stages. It moves in spirals. It unfolds in pulses. And the order it obeys is not mechanical, but organic. Not imposed from the outside, but arising from within.

This formless order is not chaos. It is not the absence of pattern. It is the presence of a deeper coherence, one that cannot always be mapped, but can be felt. It is why a flock of birds turns in unison without a leader. Why your breath finds a different rhythm in the presence of grief, or beauty, or love. Why the same set of words can feel empty in one moment and deeply alive in another. It is the underlying intelligence that connects the invisible to the visible, the unspoken to the spoken, the formless to the formed.

Most people miss this order because they are searching for something fixed. They want answers to land in neat shapes. They want timing to obey their will. But this kind of order is not something you master. It is something you attune to. And attunement begins with surrender — not to chaos, but to a greater intelligence than the one you've been taught to trust.

When you begin to feel this pulse, your orientation shifts. You stop trying to force alignment and start noticing where alignment is already present. You stop chasing certainty and begin to feel your way through movement. You become less interested in control, and more available to guidance that moves from the inside out.

The pulse of formless order is subtle. It does not override your will. It does not interrupt your choices with thunder or declarations. It whispers through sensation. It speaks in the spaces between thoughts. It nudges through synchronicity, through the feeling that something is opening or closing, not because you decided, but because a larger rhythm is unfolding.

You may feel it in the body before the mind understands it. A heaviness that says, *not now*. A lightness that says, *yes*. A tightening in the chest when something is out of sync, even if it looks perfect on the surface. Or a sense of spaciousness when you're doing something that defies logic, yet feels unmistakably right. These are not moods. They are signals. And the more you learn to trust them, the more clearly the pulse becomes.

This rhythm is not concerned with your plans. It does not ask whether something is convenient or impressive. It moves in accordance with what is most true, not what is most desired. And because of this, it often leads you into places your mind would never choose. It dismantles timelines. It disrupts expectations. It opens doors you didn't know were closed and closes the ones you clung to out of fear. But beneath all of this movement is a coherence so vast, so intelligent, that even your losses begin to carry meaning.

The pulse does not argue. It does not need your approval. It continues whether you notice it or not. But the moment you begin to feel it — not with your logic, but with your life — something changes. You begin to loosen your grip. You stop demanding constant definition. You stop measuring progress in linear terms. And in doing so, you begin to inhabit time differently. You begin to move with life, rather than against it.

This is not passivity. It is precision. You are no longer acting out of conditioning, but out of response. You speak when there is resonance. You move when the current says move. You rest when the pulse pulls you inward, even if the world insists on momentum. You begin to value the unseen alignment over the visible outcome. You begin to trust the timing of your soul more than the calendar of your culture.

This shift is subtle, but it is profound. It cannot be faked. It reveals itself in how you make decisions, in how you speak, in what you allow yourself to release. You may find yourself saying no to things that once felt essential. You may find yourself called into stillness when everything external tells you to act. You may feel the discomfort of uncertainty and choose to remain there, not because you are stuck, but because you can feel that something is gestating in the silence.

It is in that gestation that the pulse works most powerfully. It does not rush. It does not force emergence. Like the tide, it moves in cycles. Each cycle has a purpose. Each pause has a pattern. But you must listen with the whole of your being to perceive it. You must be willing to feel when something is off rhythm, even if it looks aligned from the outside. That feeling is not your doubt. It is your intelligence.

The deeper you go into this way of moving, the more you begin to see it everywhere. In the cadence of your breath. In the way truth lands in the body. In the subtle expansion or contraction of energy when you are in the presence of something real. You begin to live not by instinct alone, but by attunement. And attunement, once refined, becomes your compass.

From this place, guidance does not come as answers. It comes as alignment. You feel when you are on the beam, when your words echo the deeper frequency of your knowing. You feel when you've drifted, when your actions are no longer in rhythm with what's true. This is not about guilt or perfection. It is about return. The pulse is always inviting you back.

You are not here to follow a rigid plan. You are here to remember the design that lives beneath structure. You are not here to dominate your path. You are here to walk it in such a way that your every step is part of a greater unfolding. The pulse of formless order is not something you capture. It is something you become. And in becoming it, you dissolve the illusion that wisdom must be loud, or fast, or fixed.

It was never about controlling the pattern. It was about realizing you *are* the pattern — not as something separate from the whole, but as a single beat in the great, eternal rhythm of what has always been.

# That Which Moves All Without Moving

*At the center of every living system, there is a stillness that does not sleep. It is not passive, yet it exerts no force. It does not reach, yet it pulls. It does not act, yet through it all action becomes possible. You will not find it with the senses, and you cannot measure it with tools. And yet, it moves everything. It turns galaxies. It calls seeds upward. It breathes behind the breath. It is the silent current beneath all becoming, and it asks for nothing in return.*

---

This presence is not a being, but it is not impersonal. It is not an object, but it is not nothing. It is the ground of all things. The Taoists called it the Way. Mystics have called it the Source, the Unseen, the Nameless Light. Philosophers struggled to describe it without reducing it. Some pointed to it through paradox, others through silence. But every true tradition has known it, not as doctrine, but as direct experience.

To feel it is to become aware of what remains constant as everything else changes. The body ages. Thoughts shift. Emotions rise and fall. Relationships, beliefs, identities — all pass through. But beneath it all, something remains. It does not grow, but it contains all growth. It does not change, but it allows for all change. And when you touch it, even for a moment, the world begins to realign around that point of stillness.

Most people spend their lives circling this center, chasing after movement, mistaking motion for power. But true power does not announce itself. It does not dominate. It does not need attention. True power is what everything else depends on. The stillness at the center of the wheel is what allows the wheel to turn.

This center cannot be created. It can only be remembered. It has always been there, but you've been trained to overlook it. You've been taught to seek outside yourself, to chase light in the sky rather than feel it radiating from within. You've been told that movement is progress, that stillness is stagnation. But there is a kind of stillness that is more alive than motion. A stillness that does not resist life, but reveals its essence.

To come into contact with this still point is not to withdraw from the world. It is to see it clearly for the first time. You begin to sense the difference between what is essential and what is merely urgent. You stop reacting to every ripple on the surface and start aligning with the depth beneath. This does not make you indifferent. It makes you precise. You no longer act out of compulsion. You act from coherence.

There is a strength that comes from stillness, but it is not the strength of control. It is the strength of presence. It does not fight. It does not push. It allows all things to arise and fall without being shaken. And because it cannot be disturbed, it becomes the most reliable foundation upon which anything true can be built.

To inhabit this center is to recognize that your own being is not separate from the pulse that animates all things. You do not generate it, and yet you carry it. You do not direct it, and yet it flows through every choice you make, every word you speak, every gesture you offer. Life is not something you master by doing more. It is something you align with, moment by moment, until your presence becomes a channel through which the pulse moves naturally.

This does not mean passivity. It does not mean surrendering to circumstance or ignoring the currents that push against you. It means understanding that force is never the source of movement. The true power of this stillness is revealed in how effortlessly it guides action, how naturally it coordinates with the tides of existence. When you act from this place, your energy is efficient, your awareness sharp, your intention clear. You no longer expend effort to steer what cannot be controlled. Instead, you navigate with discernment, responding to the world with the precision of one who is tuned to its rhythm.

Every pattern you observe in nature — the turning of planets, the growth of a tree, the formation of rivers — is a reflection of this still center. It moves everything without moving itself. And as you attune to it, you begin to perceive the same dynamic in the unfolding of your own life. Obstacles are not interruptions. They are signals, opportunities to realign with the pulse beneath the apparent chaos. Challenges are not threats, but invitations to return to the source of steadiness within.

The subtlety of this presence may go unnoticed for long stretches. Its power is quiet, and often invisible to those who measure by activity or noise. But its influence is profound. It underpins creativity, informs intuition, and steadies the mind when storms of thought arise. It gives coherence to moments that would otherwise feel scattered, and it maintains continuity in the face of change. In this stillness, movement finds its integrity. Without it, motion becomes restless, disconnected, and ultimately fruitless.

To cultivate awareness of this pulse, begin by observing without interference. Notice the sensations in your body, the rhythm of your breath, the flow of thought. Allow moments of stillness to expand, not as empty gaps, but as receptive space. In these spaces, the presence of the center reveals itself naturally. It does not demand belief. It does not ask for recognition. It simply exists, waiting for your attention, ready to inform your actions and clarify your understanding.

As you deepen this practice, you realize that nothing truly moves independently. Every ripple, every wave, every shift in circumstance is orchestrated by the hidden intelligence that does not move, yet moves all. Your own life, once perceived as disjointed or unpredictable, begins to unfold with coherence. Decisions that once seemed overwhelming or uncertain become guided by an instinct that feels both intimate and vast. You begin to act in concert with something far greater than individual will, and in doing so, you discover a freedom that is grounded, not chaotic.

The center does not compete. It does not demand. It does not manipulate outcomes to suit expectation. Its influence is invisible, yet undeniable. Its presence is a reminder that true authority comes from alignment, not force. And as you allow your own being to synchronize with this pulse, you find that the world responds in kind. Tension softens. Clarity emerges. Actions resonate, and your journey becomes a reflection of the intelligence that has always been at the core of existence.

To dwell in this truth is not to escape life. It is to inhabit it fully, with awareness, precision, and grace. The pulse that moves all without moving is not a distant ideal. It is the ground beneath your feet, the quiet within your chest, the constant beneath every impermanent form. When you recognize it and live from it, you are no longer separate from the movement of life. You are its living expression, harmonized, centered, and awake.

# Chapter II: The Chamber of the Double Flame

## The Sacred Tension of the Two

*There is a force that pulls everything apart. And there is a force that draws all things back together. Between them lives the pulse of creation.*

---

We often speak of opposites as enemies. Light and dark. Masculine and feminine. Order and chaos. Mind and body. Spirit and matter. We are taught to choose one and reject the other, to elevate one as superior while demonizing the opposite. But wisdom does not live in opposition. It lives in the space between.

This space is not neutral. It is charged. It holds the power that arises when opposites are held, not resolved. When they are allowed to face each other fully without collapsing into sameness or tearing each other apart. This is sacred tension. And it is not a flaw in the structure of things. It is the very condition through which life can unfold.

Without this tension, there is no movement. Without polarity, there is no magnetism, no attraction, no ignition of transformation. It is through the dance of the two that energy arises. Not in domination, not in collapse, but in conscious relation. The ancient symbols of alchemy, tantra, and the great mystical traditions understood this. They did not seek to erase difference, but to sanctify it — to bring the two into such deep presence with each other that a third element was born from their union.

You can feel this tension in your own being. The desire for stillness, and the pull toward action. The longing to belong, and the call to remain sovereign. The urge to speak, and the ache for silence. These are not contradictions to be resolved. They are the living architecture of the human experience. You were not meant to flatten yourself into consistency. You were meant to learn how to hold the charge between what seems like opposing truths, and in that holding, to generate something deeper.

Most suffering comes not from tension itself, but from resisting it. From trying to escape into one extreme or the other. From refusing to feel the discomfort of holding both truths at once. But tension is not chaos. It is the container for revelation. When you allow the polarity within you to stay active without rushing to control it, you become capable of more refined awareness, more precise expression, more intimate connection with the intelligence that designed life this way.

The sacred tension of the two is not something you conquer. It is something you learn to relate to. You begin to sense when something is too rigid, when a polarity has been frozen into dogma or dissociation. You begin to feel when something is too loose, when meaning is lost in ambiguity or collapse. And from that sensing, you learn to inhabit the edge — not for the sake of suffering, but for the sake of power. Not control, but creative potency.

This potency is subtle. It does not erupt loudly. It rises slowly through the body, the breath, the nervous system. It becomes the quiet strength of presence. The kind that does not flinch in discomfort. The kind that can hold complexity without panic. The kind that does not need immediate resolution to stand firm in truth.

To hold this sacred tension is not to be split. It is to be widened. You are not being asked to choose between fire and water, between strength and surrender. You are being asked to become the vessel that can contain both. And in doing so, you do not dilute their essence. You deepen their potency.

The old mystics understood this. They did not seek purity by rejecting one pole of existence. They sought wholeness by integrating what was left out. They stood between heaven and earth, not as divided beings, but as bridges. They were not seeking to escape the body in favor of the spirit, nor to lose the spirit in material indulgence. They were tuning themselves to the current that flows between the two, where insight becomes flesh and flesh remembers its divine origin.

You may begin to notice this within your own inner work. As you grow more aware, you may feel parts of you that seem to move in opposite directions. One part calls for silence, another for expression. One longs for intimacy, another needs space. At first, these inner movements may seem irreconcilable. But the deeper invitation is not to resolve them prematurely. It is to stay present long enough that a third current can emerge — not compromise, but transmutation. Something altogether new, born from the holding of the two.

This is not a passive waiting. It is a conscious act. A practice of inner containment, where you allow the heat of contradiction to purify rather than divide. You begin to trust that wisdom is not born from neat answers, but from the capacity to remain whole while holding multiple truths. You begin to understand that tension is not a flaw to be removed, but a gate to deeper clarity.

In this space, something ancient returns. The memory that life is not linear, not logical in the way we've been taught. It is rhythmic. It is layered. It contains opposites not as problems, but as ingredients in a larger alchemy. Masculine and feminine. Sky and root. Expansion and return. These are not categories to be weaponized. They are frequencies to be honored, played, embodied. They are not roles to perform. They are principles that move through everything — including you.

When you resist one and over-identify with the other, you cut off half of your inheritance. You become rigid where you could have been fluid. You become overextended where you could have been anchored. But when you begin to feel both poles operating within you — when you honor their rhythm, their dialogue, their purpose — something awakens that cannot be reached by willpower alone. A deeper presence. A fuller voice. A more coherent field.

It is this coherence that begins to shape your relationships, your creations, your path. Not by simplifying your reality, but by deepening your capacity to stand within its complexity. You no longer demand that the world fit into tidy forms. You become a tuning instrument, one that can hear the harmony hidden in dissonance. You stop fearing contradiction. You begin to see it as the doorway to power.

The sacred tension of the two is not a problem to solve. It is a space to inhabit with reverence. Within it lies the key to union, not through sameness, but through conscious polarity. Not through merging, but through magnetic relationship. This is the heart of all sacred alchemy — the art of holding what seems to be opposite until it reveals the deeper wholeness from which both were born.

You are not here to collapse tension. You are here to walk its edge with awareness. To feel the fire between what pulls and what grounds. To stand in the space where creation happens — not through certainty, but through presence.

And that presence, refined in the heat of the two, becomes the portal to a new way of being. Whole. Awake. Rooted in mystery, and no longer afraid of what does not resolve.

# Fire and Water at the Heart of Creation

*At the origin of all things, two forces danced in sacred contradiction. One burned with intensity, the other flowed with depth. Fire and water — not merely elements, but living principles — came into contact and created the very fabric of what we call reality. Not in conflict, but in communion. Not in fusion, but in tension. Their relationship did not cancel either out. It gave rise to form, movement, transformation.*

---

These are not just poetic metaphors. Fire and water are encoded into everything. They are not simply outside of us, in the physical world. They live in us, through us, as us. They are woven into the architecture of energy, emotion, thought, instinct, and soul. They are not abstract opposites, but active presences. Every inner movement, every sacred ritual, every transformation of being carries their signature.

Fire is the principle of activation. It moves upward. It illuminates, consumes, refines. It is the energy of desire, of initiation, of destruction that clears the way. It brings urgency, heat, and the potential for rebirth. It is present when we take bold action, when we burn away illusion, when we feel the pressure to grow beyond what we have known. But left uncontained, fire becomes chaos. It devours what it cannot digest. It burns without purpose.

Water is the principle of receptivity. It moves downward and inward. It nourishes, cools, dissolves, remembers. It is the energy of feeling, of intuition, of depth that softens the edges. It surrounds and holds. It is present when we surrender, when we weep, when we enter the mystery without needing to understand. But left unguided, water becomes stagnation. It floods and overwhelms. It forgets its shape.

Together, they hold the blueprint of transformation. Not through domination, but through sacred interaction. One awakens, the other integrates. One expands, the other deepens. They are not meant to be balanced in a static way, but to be honored in their dynamic rhythm. They move in cycles — sometimes one leads, sometimes the other. Wisdom is not found in favoring one over the other. It is found in learning to dwell at the point of contact, where fire meets water and something new is born.

You may feel this interplay within yourself. In moments when your soul blazes with vision, yet your heart longs for stillness. In moments when your body feels the heat of urgency, while something deeper urges you to slow down and listen. These are not conflicts to be resolved, but portals to be entered. Fire and water do not agree, and they do not need to. Their friction is the source of vitality. Their contrast is what awakens the third force — the alchemical space in which true creation takes place.

Creation does not emerge from uniformity. It emerges from dynamic tension. From the spark that leaps when opposites are held without collapse. And fire and water, in their essence, carry that tension better than any other pair. One cannot replace the other. One cannot define the other. And yet, when they meet, they produce steam, transformation, movement. Not one or the other, but something entirely new.

This dance of opposites is not confined to myth or metaphor. It plays out in the felt reality of your breath, your emotions, your choices. When you feel a surge of passion or anger, that is fire rising. When you feel the ache of grief or the pull to retreat into stillness, water is descending. Each state contains wisdom. Neither is a problem to be solved. The practice is learning to read the current — to know when to let fire move and when to let water carry.

Some souls are born with more fire, burning through life with intensity. They ignite change, tear down falsehoods, speak truths that others are afraid to voice. But without water, they risk becoming consumed by their own flames, mistaking agitation for clarity, urgency for truth. Others are born with the gift of water — feeling deeply, seeing into the unseen, holding space for what others reject. But without fire, they may retreat too far inward, becoming lost in depth without direction.

To live as an initiated being is to become a vessel that can hold both. Not to extinguish one for the sake of the other, but to allow each to take its rightful place in the cycle of becoming. The teachings of the ancients never praised balance as stillness. They revered balance as motion — as the sacred turning of the wheel, the spiral of opposing forces held in intelligent motion. Every creative act mirrors this. A vision takes form in the fire of inspiration, but it must pass through the waters of gestation and refinement to become real. A spiritual insight blazes into awareness, but it must sink into the body, into practice, into ordinary life, before it transforms. The highest truths are not just those that burn with clarity. They are those that flow into life, that saturate your being like water into parched soil.

In alchemical terms, fire purifies. It strips away what is false. Water dissolves. It releases what is rigid. Together, they prepare the soul to receive new form. You do not need to force this process. You need to recognize when it is happening. When something in you is burning to be released, or when something is softening beyond your control. These are not signs of failure. They are the exact conditions under which the hidden seed begins to grow.

Sometimes, the fire will ask you to move, to speak, to cut cords, to stand alone. Sometimes, the water will ask you to feel, to yield, to hold silence, to let go of needing to know. The mystery is learning which is speaking in each moment. Not from the mind, but from the deeper pulse that lives beneath thought. The body often knows first. The breath changes. The muscles tighten or soften. The inner landscape responds long before the intellect catches up.

If you wish to walk the path of inner mastery, observe these currents as you would study the stars. Not as things to fix, but as forces to follow. Let fire awaken your power without scorching your roots. Let water soften your edges without drowning your flame. Let both reshape you until you no longer seek balance as a goal, but recognize it as the dance that never ends. In the end, creation itself is not a single act, but a rhythm. Fire and water, rising and falling, contraction and release. This rhythm is the language of the universe, and your soul is fluent in it. The more you listen, the more you remember. Not with the mind, but with the part of you that was shaped by these forces long before you were born. That part is still here, still pulsing, still remembering how to create.

## Walking the Razor's Edge of Union

*There is a place within the human experience that defies simplicity. A place where opposites meet not to clash, but to fuse into something higher. This is not the easy path of comfort or consistency. It is a path that demands presence with paradox, a path that feels like walking a razor's edge — where every step must be made with awareness, and every misstep reveals the truth you were avoiding.*

---

Union, in its most sacred form, is not a blending into sameness. It is not the melting of two into one through disappearance. It is the merging of fully embodied opposites — fierce and soft, light and dark, masculine and feminine, spirit and matter — into a dynamic whole that transcends both without denying either. This is not symbolic poetry. It is an initiatory process. It demands everything from you. And it gives back a kind of clarity that cannot be taught, only discovered.

The ancients understood this edge. In temple schools and hidden lineages, they did not teach union as an abstract ideal. They cultivated it in their initiates through tension. They placed them between forces that seemed irreconcilable — discipline and ecstasy, silence and song, action and surrender — and watched who could hold the space between without collapsing into one side. This was the real test. Not knowledge, but capacity. Not belief, but embodiment.

To walk this path today is no different. Every time you feel pulled between two truths, you are being invited into that razor's edge. Every time you want to choose either certainty or escape, you are being asked to stand instead in the middle — not frozen, but aware. Most people flee from this place. It is uncomfortable, vulnerable, uncertain. The mind wants to choose sides, to grasp one pole and reject the other. But the soul? The soul knows that real union is forged not by choosing, but by staying present where both exist.

This razor's edge is not external. It is within you. It is the line where your desire to dissolve into oneness meets your need to remain distinct. Where your longing to be held collides with your calling to walk alone. Where your intuitive knowing wrestles with your rational doubt. And each time you resist the urge to resolve the tension prematurely, something alchemical begins to occur.

This is not a path of indecision. It is a path of holding tension with reverence. Think of the bow and arrow. It is the pull of opposing forces that generates the power of the shot. Remove the tension, and the arrow falls. Deep union does not arise from avoiding tension. It arises from honoring it as sacred, from recognizing that the space between is not a void, but a crucible.

The edge can feel sharp because it cuts. It slices through false peace and exposes where you are still divided within yourself. But the wound it opens is not meant to destroy. It is meant to reveal. To tear through illusion and let the real emerge. It is a sacred wound, the kind that only truth can inflict, and only love can heal. The deeper you go, the more you realize that what you feared as separation was only preparation for union.

What begins as tension becomes rhythm. At first, the opposites within you pull in different directions, and the dissonance is loud. But as you deepen your capacity to remain open to both, something shifts. The masculine no longer silences the feminine. The rational no longer overrides the intuitive. They begin to listen to one another. They begin to move together, not in harmony born from sameness, but in unity born from sacred difference. The edge is still there, but it no longer cuts. It becomes a line of contact.

Union is not about dissolving polarity. It is about learning to hold it without fear. This is why spiritual maturity often appears as paradox to the uninitiated. The sage does not reject the world, nor is he bound by it. The priestess is both soft and untouchable. The master does not need to control, and yet everything aligns around his presence. These are not contradictions. They are signs of someone who has stopped splitting reality in half.

To live in union is not to be without conflict, but to no longer collapse under its weight. You become able to sit in the heat of it, to feel the pressure of the opposites pressing in on your heart, and to let that pressure carve you open. The ego resists this. It wants a quick resolution, a clear winner. But the soul knows that something deeper is born only when the conflict is fully embraced. The soul is not trying to escape the edge. It is trying to become it.

Most relationships falter not because love is absent, but because the razor's edge has not been honored. People come together hoping to find peace in fusion, only to discover that true intimacy asks for the opposite: the courage to remain distinct and fully seen. The closer two souls come, the sharper the edge becomes, and only those who have made peace with the tension within themselves can remain present in the tension between two. This is why sacred union, both within and with another, is not for the faint of heart. It is a devotional path. Not a path of merging into comfort, but of refining through friction.

To walk this path requires a different kind of strength. Not the force that imposes, but the presence that allows. The quiet, fierce strength of someone who will not abandon themselves in order to soothe the discomfort of complexity. This kind of strength is forged in moments when you want to collapse into one pole and instead choose to stay exactly where the discomfort lives. And in that staying, something rare is born. A still point. A moment of truth that reveals not only who you are, but what the world is made of.

Because the edge does not only exist in your inner world. It is the place where creation happens. Every great work, every act of beauty, every moment of divine inspiration is born from that space where tension is held and not fled. Art lives there. Revelation lives there. The voice of the sacred becomes audible only when the noise of resolution has quieted.

And so, to walk the razor's edge of union is to accept that wholeness is not comfort. It is not resolution. It is a presence vast enough to include all of you. All of your light, all of your shadow. All of your certainty, and all that you will never understand. It is to become the vessel in which the One expresses through the Two, not by erasing difference, but by sanctifying it. The edge is never easy. But it is holy. And the more you return to it, the more you will begin to see that this narrow path is not a burden. It is a gateway. A way back to the original rhythm. The breath before division. The pulse before time. The place where everything was already whole. And still, it moves.

# Chapter III: The Path of the Serpent and the Staff

## The Spiral Within the Spine

*The spine is more than a column of bone. It is the sacred axis of the human form, a bridge between heaven and earth, between the infinite above and the fertile depth below. In many traditions, it is known not only as an anatomical structure, but as a subtle channel—one that carries the essence of awakening. And hidden within this vertical bridge is a spiral. Not visible to the eye, yet intimately felt by those who begin to move inward.*

---

The spiral is an ancient symbol, older than written language. It appears in the shells of seasnails, in the arrangement of galaxies, in the winding of vines and weather systems. It is the signature of life's motion. Not linear, not circular, but evolving. A spiral holds paradox: it returns, but never to the same place. It curves back toward its origin, but at a higher or deeper level. It is how consciousness grows. And that same sacred geometry is woven into the human body, encoded in the way energy moves along the spine.

Most people live disconnected from this current. They move from the head down or the hips up, but rarely sense the quiet intelligence that lives between. The spine becomes mechanical, something to hold posture or endure tension. But when you begin to feel into its subtle rhythms, you discover that the spine is not stiff. It is alive. It breathes. It pulses. And most importantly, it spirals.

This spiral is not metaphorical. It is experienced directly in certain moments—during deep breath, during intimate movement, in meditation, or even in stillness. You may feel a subtle twisting motion, like a dance within the centerline of your body. Not a muscular action, but something more ancient and refined, like the memory of a serpent that once knew how to rise. In yogic systems, this is the rising of kundalini. In other paths, it is the ascent of the subtle fire. In all of them, it is a return to an inner movement that restores alignment with the sacred.

The spiral within the spine is not a force to be commanded. It cannot be summoned through effort. It responds only to awareness. To receptivity. When the mind quiets and the breath deepens, the spiral begins to make itself known—not as something you do, but as something you remember. It is already there, but veiled by the straight lines and rigid systems you've been taught to live by.

Linear thinking teaches us to move from point A to B. Spiritual teachings, too, are often consumed like this: step one, step two, result. But the spiral invites something different. It teaches us to revisit the same truths again and again, each time from a new level of depth. It is not regression. It is refinement. When you begin to perceive the spiral within your own spine, you start to live from that wisdom. You allow your growth to curve, to return, to deepen, without shame.

The spiral also teaches patience. In a world obsessed with forward momentum and speed, the spiral slows you down. It shows you that true ascent does not bypass the ground. It coils downward before it rises. It descends into the root, into the hidden, into what has been buried. And only from there does it begin to climb.

This descent is not a detour but part of the sacred architecture. Just as roots spiral deeper into the earth before a tree reaches toward the sky, so too must your awareness descend into the densest parts of your being before true elevation is possible. Many seek transcendence without embodiment. They want the crown without anchoring the root. But a spiral knows balance. It moves both ways.

When you listen deeply to the spiral, you begin to feel that the so-called blocks along the spine are not accidents. The constrictions, the pains, the tensions—they are markers. They speak in the language of sensation, alerting you to where the current cannot flow. But these are not flaws to be fixed. They are invitations. Each knot, each tightness, holds a story, often a forgotten one. And when you meet these places with breath and presence, the spiral begins to loosen them. Not by force, but by remembrance.

At the heart of many ancient traditions is the image of the serpent. Coiled at the base of the spine, resting until stirred. It is no coincidence that the serpent moves in spirals. Its awakening is not linear. It does not rise in a single burst but weaves its way upward, turning inward and around, touching each center of the self. In some stories, it is feared. In others, revered. But in all, it is a symbol of transformation. To awaken the spiral is to allow that sacred serpent to rise—not as myth, but as experience.

This rising does not always bring bliss. Sometimes it brings heat. Sometimes tears. Sometimes a trembling as the body remembers what it once knew before the world told it to forget. The nervous system must adjust. The mind must quiet. The ego must soften its grip. The spiral will not move through force, but it also will not tolerate falsehood. It clears what no longer belongs. It dissolves what is stagnant. And it reveals what is true.

To live from the spiral is to live with reverence for subtlety. It is to walk through life sensing more than you analyze. It is to feel how every interaction, every movement, every breath is part of a larger choreography. You begin to notice how even your thoughts follow patterns. How your emotions spiral toward their roots before they release. You no longer see yourself as broken. You see yourself as unfolding.

The body becomes your scripture. The spine your scroll. And the spiral the ink that writes the story of awakening from within. There is a dignity that returns when you recognize this. You no longer seek outside for the key. You become the key. You are no longer desperate to escape. You realize that the entire path was already encoded in the sacred geometry of your being.

There are moments when the spiral reveals its silence. A stillness so vast it contains every motion. A center so unmoving that all movement seems to originate from it. This is the point around which the spiral turns. The eye within the motion. The mystery that never changes even as everything else dances around it. In those moments, you know yourself not as the body that carries the spiral, but as the spiral itself. Not as the seeker, but as the path.

And from there, something quiet and profound begins to guide you. Not with loud visions or dramatic signs, but with subtle currents. You begin to move through the world with a different rhythm. Less rushed. Less fragmented. More attuned. You know when to rise, when to root, when to turn inward, and when to expand. Life becomes less about achievement and more about alignment. Less about arrival and more about attunement to the spiral's next curve.

The sacred is no longer distant. It is curled within you, waiting to be lived.

# The Coiled Light at the Base

*Beneath all thought, beneath all striving, beneath the movement of the breath itself, there is a still place where something ancient waits. Not passive, not forgotten, but quietly alive. Coiled. This presence at the base of your spine is not merely metaphor. It is a living intelligence, a current of primordial energy that has been encoded into your very structure. It waits not to be forced, but to be remembered.*

---

Every sacred tradition that speaks in symbols carries this thread. In the East, it is Kundalini, the serpent-fire resting at the root. In the mysteries of Kemet, it is the uraeus, the serpent rising upon the brow of the initiate, awakened from its coiled slumber. In the Hebrew scriptures, it is the Shekinah, the indwelling radiance. And even in the unspoken rituals of indigenous lineages, there is the knowing of something hidden and potent, rooted in the body and guarding the threshold of true power.

What makes this force sacred is not just its intensity, but its precision. It does not flood indiscriminately. It rises through alignment. It responds to rhythm, breath, truth. It knows when the body is ready and when the psyche is steady enough to receive what it carries. This light is not separate from your consciousness, but it is not your conscious mind. It belongs to the deeper architecture of being, the layer beneath the personal story.

Many have tried to summon it prematurely. They force breath, strain poses, chase ecstatic states. But the coiled light cannot be tricked. It does not answer to desperation. It listens for sincerity. It opens only when the soil of the self has been tilled and the roots of fear have been acknowledged. This is not a performance for the world. This is a sacred homecoming.

At the base of the spine lies not only the seed of physical life, but also the memory of every survival instinct you have ever known. Fear, contraction, defensiveness—all live here too. The same center that stores your primal memories also holds the gateway to your transformation. This is why the process is not merely energetic. It is emotional. It is existential. To awaken the coiled light is to face every layer of what you have stored in the dark.

It may begin subtly. A warmth that lingers longer than usual at the base of your pelvis. A sense of pressure or tingling along the spine during stillness. A dream that shakes loose an old memory. A moment where your breath moves you without your control. These are not signs to chase, but signals to honor. The energy does not rise by effort. It rises by invitation.

There is an intelligence in the design. The light is coiled not just downward, but inward. Like the spiral of galaxies or the unfurling of a fern, it follows a sacred geometry. As it begins to stir, it touches every layer of your being. Not just chakra by chakra in a linear ascent, but through a multidimensional unfolding. You are not simply a ladder to be climbed, but a temple to be illuminated.

The body knows how to contain this. It was built for it. But it must be listened to. If there is trauma stored in the tissues, the light will surface it. If there are patterns that no longer serve, the light will dismantle them. Not out of cruelty, but because it is purification. The coiled light does not rise to impress. It rises to transform.

Let yourself feel the gravity of this. The base is not something to transcend, but to reclaim. This is where your roots meet the sacred. This is the place where survival meets soul. And it is from this place that the real ascent begins—not by leaving the body behind, but by entering it fully.

To enter the body fully is to consent to its language. The sensations at the base are not merely physical—they are thresholds. Each tension, each pulse, each subtle contraction around the pelvic floor or lower back is a form of communication. This light responds to presence, not performance. It asks you to inhabit your own foundation with reverence.

There is a sacred reason why the root is the starting point. Before you can speak truth, you must stand on it. Before you can rise into higher vision, you must be grounded in what is real. The coiled light does not awaken through fantasy but through contact—contact with the breath, the bones, the blood, the unspoken fears and ancestral echoes that live within your lower body. This is not the realm of quick rewards. It is the deep, slow work of integration.

You are not here to bypass the primal, but to sanctify it. The instincts of the root are not obstacles to overcome, but raw, untouched aspects of your sacred design. When you begin to meet these places—not with judgment, but with intimacy—they begin to soften. The light does not push them aside. It weaves through them, reshaping them from within.

This is why devotion matters. Not to a teacher or system, but to the process itself. A steady, humble relationship with your own body's intelligence creates the conditions for emergence. The light at the base is not yours to control, but it will move through you when the vessel becomes coherent enough to hold its power. It needs your honesty more than your technique. It requires your listening more than your effort.

There is a quiet beauty in the early stages of awakening. They are often overlooked in favor of dramatic expressions. But it is in these first stirrings—in the stillness before the ascent, in the subtle shifts of inner space—that the most profound recalibrations occur. Your breath may deepen without instruction. Your spine may adjust itself without conscious correction. You may feel a clarity that was not learned but remembered. This is the body responding to the presence of something ancient, something sacred.

As the coiled light begins to ascend, it does not do so in a straight line. It moves according to a spiral, a rhythm that transcends logic. Sometimes it rises and pauses. Sometimes it descends before climbing again. These movements are not regressions. They are recalibrations. The energy is mapping a new alignment in your system. It is not a staircase but a living current, and the only way to stay attuned to it is through presence.

Every awakening must pass through the gate of the base. It is the keeper of memory, the guardian of truth, the temple of potential. If there is fear, the light will meet it. If there is shame, the light will illuminate it. If there is power hidden beneath suppression, the light will call it forth. What rises from here is not just energy—it is identity reformed, awareness renewed, will clarified.

You are not separate from this force. You are its expression. And as you honor its timing, its wisdom, its slow unfolding, you begin to realize that the journey of awakening is not a chase toward the divine, but a surrender to it. The sacred does not descend from the heavens. It emerges from within, coiled in silence, waiting for the moment your attention becomes worship. Let this part of you be felt. Not just known, not just observed, but inhabited. When the light begins to rise, let it teach you what no words can convey. Let it reveal the truth encoded in your spine, your breath, your blood. And let it remind you that the root was never a place to escape, but the threshold of return.

# Commanding Without Force, Rising Without Strain

*There is a kind of power that does not announce itself. It does not clench its fists or shout to be heard. It moves in stillness, and yet its presence shifts the entire field. This power does not need to control anything because it is already aligned with the deeper currents that move all things. It does not command through domination, but through coherence. It is not reactive, but responsive. This is the power of spiritual authority that arises when inner contradiction dissolves and the being becomes undivided.*

---

To command without force is not to abdicate strength, but to wield a subtler, more intelligent form of it. It is the power of presence that shapes reality from the inside. It is rooted in clarity, not aggression. In trust, not tension. The old paradigm taught us that to have impact we must push, manipulate, strategize. But the deeper current reveals another way. When your energy is attuned to truth, when your actions are synchronized with something larger than personal will, you begin to affect the world without needing to strain against it.

This kind of movement feels like grace. You are not driven, but drawn. You are not exhausting yourself to make things happen. You are moving with a current, and that current responds to your alignment. The more inner force you try to apply from the mind, the more resistance you often create. But when you release the compulsion to control outcomes, and instead embody the frequency of what is true, things begin to reorganize around you. Not always instantly, but inevitably.

To rise without strain requires a deep restructuring of how you relate to power, success, even to effort. The path does not ask for passivity, but for precision. You are still required to show up, to choose, to act. But you are not climbing from lack. You are rising from remembrance. The energy that animates creation already lives in you. It is not something to conquer, but to uncover.

Many teachings have spoken of surrender, but often in ways that feel abstract. What does it mean, practically, to surrender and still act in the world? It means to let go of the inner tension that assumes you must force life to cooperate. It means to tune yourself like an instrument, so that when you speak, move, or create, it is not from desperation or over-effort, but from a clean, undistorted signal. Surrender is not passivity. It is conscious alignment.

At this level, force becomes noise. Strain becomes interference. You begin to notice how certain desires were not truly yours, but inherited templates of what you were told mattered. You start recognizing how much of your energy was being used to chase a version of power that was externally defined. And you start to pull that energy back, not to retreat, but to refine. What remains is a quieter, more stable flame.

You learn to hold your center even when things around you are uncertain. You do not seek to overpower, but to emanate. Your presence becomes a field, not a reaction. And that field begins to speak before you do. People sense it. Situations bend subtly toward it. You're no longer trying to convince the world of your worth. You are simply living in accordance with it. The world begins to reflect that internal coherence without the need for constant negotiation.

The more deeply you root into this quiet power, the more you realize that much of what you once believed was necessary was only noise. Urgency begins to fade. You no longer feel the need to constantly prove or explain. Your actions arise not from mental calculation, but from a still inner certainty. What to say, what to do, what to walk away from — all of it becomes simpler. Not always easier, but cleaner.

This clarity doesn't come from passively waiting. It emerges through discipline, through tending to the internal terrain where the noise is born. Old patterns of proving, defending, or chasing are not easily dissolved. They may resurface again and again, especially when you are met with uncertainty. But you begin to meet them not with struggle, but with inquiry. You begin to ask, "What part of me still believes it must strain to be heard? What part still fears it is not enough?"

These questions do not demand quick answers. They open space. And within that space, new configurations of being emerge. Not identities or postures, but inner architectures that are more stable, more sovereign. This is what it means to rise without strain: you are not lifting yourself with borrowed tools or borrowed voices. You are rising from your own ground. The force is not added to you. It comes from the dissolving of what was in the way.

Sometimes this feels like stillness. Sometimes like fire. But it is never frantic. It has no interest in performance. Even your ambition becomes purified. It no longer seeks to escape the present or accumulate symbols of power. It turns into a longing to embody truth more fully, more precisely. Your desire becomes simpler. To be aligned. To be useful. To live and act from the deepest intelligence available to you.

You start noticing a pattern: the more you let go of forcing, the more life begins to cooperate. This is not a promise of ease, but of harmony. Challenges may still appear, but they no longer feel like punishment. They become mirrors, invitations to step further into coherence. You stop pushing doors that will not open and start standing before the ones that are already ajar. Your timing sharpens. You act when it's time, and not a moment before.

You also become less reactive. Not numb, not distant, but composed. When others are caught in drama, your clarity becomes a stabilizing presence. When others expect you to fight or prove, your refusal becomes a quiet revolution. You are no longer playing the same game. And people feel it. Some will misunderstand. Some will resist it. But others will recognize something they forgot they were allowed to be.

True spiritual authority does not come from claiming superiority. It arises from emptiness, from transparency. It doesn't seek credit. It doesn't crave attention. And yet it reshapes the field. When you are no longer trying to grasp, you can finally hold. When you are no longer desperate to rise, you begin to ascend in ways that cannot be explained or replicated.

You begin to trust that your presence is enough. You are not here to overpower life, but to participate in its unfolding with clarity and devotion. And from this place, you do not shrink, you do not puff up. You move with precision, speak with weight, act with timing. You let life rise through you, not around you.

This is the mystery: that the less you try to control, the more command you seem to have. Not over others, but over the quality of energy you bring into the world. That is the truest form of influence. And it cannot be faked. It can only be remembered, refined, and finally embodied.

# Chapter IV: The Hidden Geometry of the Soul

## The Pattern That Cannot Be Seen

*There is a structure beneath all things. Not the visible one, shaped by matter and motion, but something more elusive. It does not draw attention to itself, yet it governs what unfolds. It is the framework behind the seen, the silent architecture that organizes existence without needing to announce its presence. It does not ask to be noticed. It simply is.*

---

To the eye trained only in surfaces, the world appears fragmented. Random events, disconnected choices, accidents and chaos. But the deeper eye begins to perceive an intelligence moving through it all. Not a mechanical plan, nor a script already written, but a subtle coherence that reveals itself only when we stop insisting on controlling it. This is the pattern that cannot be seen. Not because it is absent, but because it is too vast, too fine, too alive to be grasped through ordinary sight.
Mystics across cultures have spoken of it in different ways. The Tao, the Logos, the Net of Indra, the Book of Life, the Akashic Field. Each term attempts to point to the same truth: there is something that holds the multiplicity together. It is not rigid. It breathes. And yet it holds a kind of lawfulness that is beyond human law. When you begin to live in harmony with it, things move. When you live against it, things resist. It is not punishing you. It is not rewarding you. It is simply responding to resonance. But the pattern cannot be forced to reveal itself. It is not decoded through cleverness or analysis. It opens through attunement. Through humility. Through a willingness to step outside the mind's need to categorize and control. The intellect can map many things, but this pattern lives beyond maps. It slips between the lines of the logical. It is known through the body, through the felt sense, through the quiet recognition that something deeper is guiding the unfolding — if we would only stop interrupting it.
We often miss it because we are trained to look for straight lines, clear outcomes, and immediate results. The deeper pattern moves in spirals, in echoes, in slow convergences. It does not obey the timelines we impose. It

arranges events not for efficiency, but for revelation. It teaches through experience, not explanation. Its wisdom is sometimes wrapped in silence, sometimes in loss, sometimes in the absurd timing of things falling apart just before they fall together.

You cannot manipulate this pattern, but you can align with it. And alignment begins with listening. Not to the noise of your preferences, but to the subtle signals that life sends when you are quiet enough to notice. The body knows. The breath knows. The dreams that come uninvited in the middle of the night often know. They speak a language the conscious mind cannot translate, but the soul understands it clearly.

As you begin to walk in greater sensitivity, you may notice moments where something clicks into place without your effort. A meeting that changes everything. A phrase you needed to hear spoken by a stranger. A delay that saved your life. The more you pay attention, the more these moments no longer feel random. They feel like glimpses of a thread running beneath the visible, stitching together a deeper story that your surface life is only beginning to reflect.

These are not moments to be dramatized. They are to be honored. They are signs that the unseen pattern is working with you, drawing you inward, asking you to move not just from strategy but from alignment. At a certain point, you stop asking whether you are making the right choice and start asking whether you are moving in truth. That becomes the only compass that matters.

The question is not whether the pattern exists. The question is whether we are still enough to feel its rhythm. In a world saturated with noise, urgency, and fragmented attention, this capacity has become rare. Yet it has never been more needed. The pattern is not a secret because it is hidden behind walls, but because we have forgotten how to sit in the stillness required to perceive it.

When we return to the ancient ways of knowing, we find that this pattern was always central. It guided planting seasons and ritual cycles. It was etched into temples and sung into chants. Not as superstition, but as living alignment with what is. The elders did not need data to know when to move, when to speak, when to wait. Their alignment was not accidental. It came from intimacy with the unseen.

To enter that intimacy today requires a stripping away of distraction, a softening of the insistence to always know. It demands an inner silence fierce enough to withstand the pull of ego's certainty. The pattern does not speak in the voice of fear. It does not flatter or dominate. It whispers. It repeats itself until we are ready to receive. Sometimes it breaks us open just enough to make us porous to it again.

There is no formula for seeing it, only refinement. And this refinement is not an act of ambition. It is an act of devotion. To walk in harmony with the unseen is not to live without challenge, but to live with coherence. Even suffering begins to carry a different fragrance. You no longer view it as punishment, but as re-alignment. Life corrects the course when you veer away from the rhythm. Not to harm, but to bring you back into resonance. As the inner field becomes more still, the outer events begin to mirror that stillness. This is not about passivity or escape. It is about anchored presence. You move in the world, but not from the same place. You speak, but from a current deeper than opinion. You act, but no longer from frantic momentum. You become a vessel through which the pattern expresses itself in real time. Not by imposing, but by allowing.

This allowing is a form of spiritual maturity. It means learning to navigate not with control, but with clarity. You may still make plans, but you hold them lightly. You pay attention to resistance, not as failure, but as feedback. You release the need to constantly push forward and begin to let life reveal when and how to move. The path becomes less linear, more alive. And strangely, more effective.

Those who walk this way are not loud. They do not gather attention through spectacle. But there is a quiet power around them. You feel it in their presence, not in what they say, but in how they listen. Not in what they achieve, but in how they align. They do not try to stand out. They try to stay true. Their lives begin to resemble the unseen pattern itself: coherent, meaningful, unforced.

When you live like this, you begin to remember something ancient. You realize that life was never meant to be figured out like a puzzle. It was meant to be entered like a ceremony. The pattern is not a problem to solve. It is a presence to honor. The moment you stop trying to conquer it and start offering yourself to it, it begins to speak through you. Not with volume, but with truth.

And if you trust it long enough, you will begin to see that the events you once questioned were never accidents. The delays, the detours, the doors that closed — all of it was speaking in the language of the unseen. All of it was preparing you for the alignment you now carry. You were never off the path. You were being shaped by it.

The pattern cannot be held in the hand, but it can be lived in the body. And once you feel it moving through you, you will never again mistake chaos for disorder. You will know that even in the darkest moments, something wiser is weaving the threads. Not because you deserve it. Not because you earned it. But because you are part of it. Always have been. Always will be.

## Sigils Etched in Ether

*There are markings that do not fade with time. They are not carved into stone, not inked onto flesh, not bound to any visible matter. Yet they exist with a clarity more enduring than iron, more precise than script. These are the sigils etched in ether — patterns born of intention, shaped by will, and set into the subtle fabric of reality.*

---

A sigil is not merely a symbol. It is a convergence point between thought, frequency, and form. In ancient traditions, sigils were crafted by mystics who understood that the invisible realms respond not to language alone, but to resonance. To etch something in ether is to imprint a vibration upon the unseen, to create a kind of living code that aligns reality with the will of its author.

But to speak of will in this context requires refinement. This is not egoic will, not the desperate striving of personality. It is the will that arises from stillness, from inner clarity, from alignment with the deeper current of life. The sigils born from this place are not tools of manipulation, but of communion. They do not command reality through force, but invite it into harmony through pattern.

When the ancients created sigils, they did not rush. Each line, curve, and stroke was a gesture of consecration. The form mattered, yes, but it was the intent behind the form that gave it power. The act of creation was a ritual in itself — a wordless dialogue between inner knowing and outer gesture. The symbol was not the spell; it was the vessel. The true spell was the resonance it carried, the frequency it summoned into being.

In the ether, these frequencies do not dissipate as sound does. They linger, like light across water, like scent in the folds of cloth. This is why sacred places hum long after the rituals cease. This is why some objects seem to radiate presence. The ether holds what has been offered to it with clarity. It does not forget. When a sigil is impressed into that field with clarity, it becomes a living architecture, drawing experience into alignment with the code it carries.

Modern minds often dismiss this as superstition, or reduce it to mere psychology. But the field of life is more subtle than either dogma or data can capture. It is shaped not only by action, but by orientation — by the quality of attention and the coherence of intent. A properly created sigil is not a superstition; it is a signature left upon the current of the unseen, like a seal impressed upon wax before it hardens.

The alchemists knew this. So did the desert mystics, the forest seers, the temple scribes. They did not rely on belief alone. They tested, observed, refined. They learned that certain combinations of sound, shape, and silence could influence the patterns of emergence. They understood that sigils are not static images, but dynamic codes. Not decorations, but doorways.

Even today, we are surrounded by them — corporate logos mimicking ancient glyphs, state emblems echoing temple seals, language itself fragmented from its primal power. Much of this is unconscious now, weaponized in reverse, turned toward distraction and dissonance. But beneath that noise, the original current still flows, and the art of conscious sigil work remains.

To return to this path is to reclaim the capacity to imprint meaning onto the invisible. Not for spectacle, but for sanctity. Not to bend the world to our preference, but to inscribe our soul's coherence into the field around us. And when that inscription is true — when it arises from a place of devotion rather than distortion — the ether listens. It always has.

The sigil that endures is not one made in haste or from mental grasping. It is born in the stillness behind thought, at the crossing of intuition and silence. That is why it cannot be manufactured through formulas or copied from ancient books without inner alignment. The outer symbol is only ever a fingerprint of something deeper. To create a sigil that moves reality is to enter into resonance with the force that shaped the cosmos itself.

This is not metaphor. It is an esoteric truth hidden in plain sight. The creative field that gives birth to stars, cells, and symphonies is governed by harmonic proportion. It responds to integrity, clarity, and deep coherence. When a symbol is infused with these elements, it begins to carry a charge — a kind of subtle magnetism that draws toward it the echo of its own frequency. This is how a simple shape etched on paper, if created in alignment with a deep enough current, can begin to bend the probabilities around it.

But this is not a tool for the impatient or the prideful. The ether responds to what we are, not what we pretend. If one's field is clouded by confusion or unconscious contradiction, no amount of artistic perfection will compensate. A sigil is an extension of being. It reveals the state of the one who created it, not just the desire. To inscribe a false intention — to seek power from separation — is to etch distortion into the ether, which only multiplies dissonance.

This is why the old mystics cleansed themselves before creation. Not for superstition, but to clarify their field, to become a pure conduit for that which wished to be expressed. They knew that sacred symbols are not chosen arbitrarily. They emerge. The truest sigils are not invented; they are remembered. They rise from the depths of the unconscious like dreams that carry truth. They are shaped by forces that whisper from beyond the veil of language.

When the practitioner is in harmony with this emergence, the result is not just a symbol but a mirror. It reflects the architecture of the soul's alignment with the whole. It vibrates subtly through the layers of perception and imprints itself upon the invisible scaffolding of experience. It becomes not just an artistic act, but a kind of energetic encryption — a seal of presence that continues to reverberate long after the pen is lifted.

There are those who speak of activation, of awakening dormant codes within the self. A true sigil, born of right alignment, does exactly that. It does not add something foreign. It unlocks what was already waiting. It reminds the inner world of what it already knows. It is a key that fits not because it forces, but because it was shaped by the same geometry as the lock itself.

And so the practice of sigil work becomes a form of internal alchemy. Not a method of control, but a path of precision. The one who learns to inscribe the ether is not playing with superstition. They are speaking the silent language of emergence. They are engaging in a sacred dialogue with the formless field that shapes all things. They are no longer merely reacting to life but participating in its unfolding with intelligence and reverence.

This does not require ornate rituals or public declarations. Some of the most potent symbols are etched in the mind, carved in breath, or traced silently in the space between thoughts. The external form is only the echo. What matters is the frequency behind it. The clarity of presence. The purity of will. The willingness to become so empty that the symbol does not come from you, but through you.

In the end, the sigil is not separate from the one who creates it. It is a crystallization of their essence, a vibration distilled into form. And once released into the ether, it begins to work — not as magic in the vulgar sense, but as alignment. It adjusts the field, softens resistance, and opens space for what is already true to emerge.

The mystic does not chase results. They craft the sigil, offer it into the unseen, and return to stillness. They know the ether does not forget. What is etched with presence remains. What is cast with clarity resounds. And in that sacred imprint, a new pattern begins to unfold — not forced, not grasped, but remembered.

# Aligning the Inner Temple to the Divine Grid

*The concept of the "inner temple" has been spoken of across traditions, often veiled in allegory. It is not a place built of stone or wood, but a field of living awareness formed by coherence, integrity, and devotion. To align this inner temple to the Divine Grid is not merely a symbolic act. It is a sacred task that requires precision, willingness, and clarity of orientation.*

---

The Divine Grid refers to the unseen structure underlying reality. It is the intelligent framework through which all manifestation flows — the hidden geometry of life. It is not static, nor is it a mechanical pattern. It pulses with intelligence, with rhythm, with responsiveness. When the inner temple is aligned with this grid, the human being becomes more than a seeker. They become a resonant node in the fabric of creation, an awakened conduit through which wisdom, energy, and purpose can move without distortion.

This alignment is not accomplished by belief or blind imitation. It is realized through a deep reordering of the inner architecture. The mind, emotions, body, and subtle systems must begin to attune themselves to something beyond preference or egoic will. This is not a self-denial, but a self-offering — a movement from fragmentation to unity.

At the core of this process is sincerity. Alignment is not a performance. It is not gained by presenting the outer self as spiritual or disciplined while the inner world remains in chaos or contradiction. The Divine Grid cannot be tricked. It responds to what is true, not what is claimed. Therefore, the first step toward alignment is a quiet and often humbling inner audit. Where am I out of rhythm? Where do I act from fear rather than clarity? What distortions have I inherited or constructed that interfere with my ability to sense the deeper order?

This inquiry is not meant to produce guilt or shame. It is the sacred beginning of precision. Just as an instrument must be tuned before it can join the orchestra, the inner temple must be refined so it can resonate with the vast harmony of the grid. This requires presence, attention, and an inner stillness that is not passivity but receptivity.

The process is not linear. One does not "achieve" alignment once and for all. It is a relationship, a living attunement that deepens as one's being becomes more transparent, more honest, more surrendered to truth. At times, the misalignments are subtle: a small compromise in integrity, a habitual reaction, a clinging to control. At other times, the misalignments are vast and obvious, shaking the foundations of identity itself. In both cases, the invitation is the same: return to center, return to truth, return to rhythm.

The inner temple is constructed through daily acts. Not necessarily rituals in the ceremonial sense, though those can help, but in the quality of one's attention, the clarity of one's choices, and the orientation of one's heart. Do I speak from alignment? Do I listen from stillness? Do I act from a deeper knowing or from a restless need to control? Each of these is a building block in the structure of the inner temple.

There is a moment — often quiet, almost imperceptible — when something shifts. The inner and outer begin to reflect one another. Life becomes less of a battlefield and more of a dialogue. Synchronicities increase, not because of luck, but because the field is now responsive to what is true within. Energy is no longer wasted in inner resistance. Purpose becomes less about ambition and more about alignment with something larger, something ancient, something alive.

It is at this point that a deeper architecture begins to emerge — one that cannot be imposed but only revealed.

The emerging structure is not visible in the traditional sense. It is perceived inwardly, like a silent recognition, a knowing that does not pass through the usual channels of thought. The inner temple begins to reflect the elegance of the Divine Grid not because it copies it, but because it surrenders to it. And in this surrender, something extraordinary happens: the laws of separation begin to dissolve. One no longer feels like a fragment in a vast, incomprehensible universe. Instead, there is a lived sense of participation in something vast and intimate at once.

This is not a philosophy. It is a state of being. When a person enters alignment, their presence changes. There is a coherence in their voice, a stillness behind their eyes, a grounded current beneath their movements. They no longer need to assert themselves, because their being is already registered in the field. The world begins to respond to them not out of fear or persuasion, but out of resonance. This is why alignment is more powerful than control. It does not coerce. It invites, and in that invitation lies a magnetism that cannot be faked.

The great initiates of old were not powerful because of their knowledge alone. They carried alignment in their breath, in their silence, in the structure of their attention. They had refined their inner temple to such a degree that it became a mirror of the unseen architecture. Their thoughts, words, and actions did not conflict with one another. They had become instruments finely tuned to the sacred grid, and through that alignment, they could move energies, open pathways, dissolve illusions.

To move in that way requires discipline, but not the kind that is often associated with asceticism or self-denial. It is the discipline of constant honesty, the refusal to act from incoherence, the quiet courage to listen to the deeper rhythm even when the surface demands something else. It is not about perfection. It is about fidelity. One returns, again and again, to that still place where the alignment is felt — not as a rule, but as a truth too pure to ignore.

Over time, the sensation of dissonance becomes unbearable. One cannot lie, not because of morality, but because it is physically painful to speak what is not true. One cannot act in ways that fragment the self, because the inner temple resists distortion. There is a growing sensitivity to the grid, to its symmetry, its pulse, its guidance. This sensitivity is not fragility. It is strength born from clarity. It is power without violence.

And yet, this process is not meant to lead to isolation. The inner temple, once aligned, becomes a place of communion. It is where the voice of the deeper world is heard, where insight arises without effort, where decisions come not from calculation but from recognition. From this place, service becomes natural. The aligned being does not need to seek purpose. They become purpose in motion.

There are moments in the journey when alignment seems to disappear, when confusion clouds the inner senses. These are not failures. They are calls to return. The grid does not punish. It waits. It does not demand obedience. It offers orientation. It is a compass for those who are willing to quiet the noise and feel again. Even in silence, it speaks.

The inner temple is never fully finished. It is alive, evolving, deepening. Each new layer of clarity uncovers another level of subtle alignment. The Divine Grid is vast. Its geometry expands far beyond the edges of comprehension. But even a partial alignment, even a single moment of pure resonance, can alter the trajectory of a life. Because in that moment, the individual becomes whole. Not through accumulation, but through coherence.

To walk this path is not to escape the world, but to re-enter it differently. One speaks differently, listens differently, chooses differently. The outer world may not understand, but it begins to shift in response. Life becomes less about seeking and more about revealing. Less about effort, more about precision. The inner temple becomes a sanctuary not only for the self, but for those who come near. Not because of what is said, but because of what is carried in silence.

This is alignment. Not a destination, but a living relationship. Not a structure imposed from outside, but a sacred architecture revealed from within. The Divine Grid is already present. The work is not to reach it, but to remember it, and to refine the temple until the remembering becomes permanent. Then, action is no longer reaction. It is participation. It is creation aligned with the source.

# Chapter V: The Waters That Remember

## The Body as a Vessel of Memory

*The body is not merely flesh and function. It is a living archive, an instrument of remembrance. Beneath the visible layers of skin, bone, and muscle lies a silent intelligence that carries the imprints of every experience, every choice, every trauma and triumph that has shaped a life. But it goes deeper than the memory of this lifetime alone. The body also holds the echoes of lineage, of ancestry, of ancient patterns passed down through blood, breath, and gesture. It is not just personal. It is ancestral, collective, archetypal.*

---

Long before words were used to record history, memory was passed through the body. The tilt of the head, the way one touches the earth, the rhythm of breath in moments of fear or wonder — all of these became conduits for carrying knowledge across generations. The body knows things the mind has forgotten. It remembers the way a grandparent held grief, the way a tribe honored fire, the way a child once danced before learning shame. This knowledge is not metaphorical. It is tangible, stored in fascia, muscle, and posture. It expresses itself in habits that make no rational sense, in reactions that feel disproportionate, in dreams that leave a trace in the chest. To awaken to the body as a vessel of memory is not to treat it as a problem to be fixed or an object to be sculpted. It is to enter into relationship with it as a living library. Each sensation becomes a page. Each pattern of tension becomes a paragraph. Each spontaneous movement, a line of poetry written by something older than thought. When one begins to listen in this way, the body stops being a burden. It becomes a teacher.
There is a reason why, in many ancient traditions, initiates were trained not only in philosophy but in movement. Sacred dance, breathwork, postural alignment — these were not accessories to wisdom. They were expressions of it. Because certain truths cannot be understood until they are felt in the bones. The intellect may grasp an idea, but until the body confirms it, the idea remains incomplete. This is why transformation is not mental alone.

One can read a thousand sacred texts and still remain unchanged. But a single moment of embodied recognition can rearrange an entire life.

The body is also where distortions are revealed. When the mind lies, the body tenses. When the soul is ignored, the body aches. Illness, fatigue, chronic tightness — these are not merely biological failures. They are messages. They speak in the only language the body knows: sensation. To learn to listen is not to overanalyze, but to attune. Often, what we call pain is a form of remembering. A place where something long buried is trying to surface, to be seen, to be released.

This is not to suggest that every discomfort has a mystical cause. But it is to suggest that the body always has something to say. And often, it speaks with greater clarity than the mind. In times of deep confusion, when thought becomes a maze, the body still knows. It knows when to lean in and when to pull back. It knows the difference between what feels true and what feels forced. It is a compass hidden in plain sight.

To honor the body as a vessel of memory requires a different kind of attention. Not the obsessive attention of image and performance, but the quiet, reverent attention of listening. It means asking not what the body looks like, but what it carries. What it has protected. What it still longs to express. Often, the body waits years to be heard. It waits in silence until a moment of presence arrives — not dramatic, not ceremonial, but honest.

Presence is the key that unlocks these silent stories. Not the forced kind of presence that demands effort, but the soft one that arrives when we stop fleeing. When we stop trying to transcend, fix, or explain. When we breathe deeply into the discomfort and allow the body to speak in its own rhythm, without interruption. In those moments, a different intelligence takes over. It is not analytical. It does not argue. It simply reveals.

Sometimes this revelation comes as a tremor in the chest, a tear without a reason, a sigh that seems to come from another century. These are not meaningless. They are openings. They mark the return of what was once exiled. Memory, in its purest form, is not conceptual. It is vibrational. When a memory resurfaces through the body, it does not come as a narrative but as a shift. And that shift can change everything. It can rewire perception, soften judgment, restore connection.

To walk this path requires a willingness to be deeply honest. The body does not pretend. It has no social mask. It does not perform for approval. It tightens when we betray ourselves. It opens when we align. Every time we override its signals, we build distance between our awareness and our truth. But when we return to its messages with humility, the gap begins to close. And in that narrowing space, something ancient stirs.

There is an intelligence in the body that knows the way home. It does not need to be taught. It needs to be trusted. That trust is built not through control, but through surrender. Not a passive kind of surrender, but an active participation in the conversation. Listening not just with the ears, but with the skin, the gut, the pulse. Over time, the body becomes less reactive and more expressive. It no longer needs to shout through pain or dysfunction. It can whisper. It can guide.

There is also a creative dimension to this process. As old memories rise and release, new capacities emerge. The body is not just a repository of what has been. It is a vessel for what can be. When cleared of what it has held too long, it begins to channel. It becomes a bridge between form and formlessness. This is why in some lineages, the body is referred to as a temple. Not as metaphor, but as fact. A place where the sacred can dwell. Where spirit can take shape.

In this way, healing is not just about recovery. It is about reawakening. It is about restoring the original blueprint beneath the accumulated noise. Not returning to some mythical purity, but allowing the body's own wisdom to reorganize us from within. This reorganization is not mechanical. It is alchemical. It is not achieved through force. It unfolds through attention, softness, and the courage to feel what was once unfelt.

Many seek transcendence by leaving the body, by denying it or escaping it in the name of the spiritual. But true elevation does not bypass the body. It roots more deeply into it. The higher frequencies, the refined states of awareness, require an anchor. The body is that anchor. Without it, vision floats without embodiment. Intuition flares without integration. The sacred must be carried in form if it is to shape the world.

When we begin to live from this place — where body and awareness are no longer at odds but are allies — life itself becomes different. Movement becomes prayer. Stillness becomes revelation. Every gesture becomes an offering to presence. And the body, far from being a limit, becomes a doorway. Not because it is perfect, but because it is real. Because it remembers. Because it holds the codes of return.

What has been hidden can be reclaimed. What has been buried can rise. Not through force, not through intellectual mastery, but through the quiet, rhythmic wisdom of the body itself. It knows the way. All it asks is that we learn to listen.

# The Moon's Secret in the Blood

*There is a rhythm beneath the noise of modern life that never stopped pulsing. A silent tide that pulls at the bones, the cells, the hidden places of the body. This rhythm is lunar. It governs the tides of the sea and the subtle tides within the blood. For centuries, mystics, healers, and seers understood that the moon does not merely illuminate the night sky. It speaks in frequencies that the intellect cannot hear, but the body can feel.*

---

The ancients knew the blood was not just biology. It was memory, power, and transmission. Blood was seen as a sacred river within the human temple, carrying the imprints of lineage, the echoes of choices made, and the seeds of what could yet become. And within this river, the moon was a silent conductor. Not metaphorically, but literally. The gravitational pull of the moon stirs not only oceans but the fluids within our own vessels. This movement is not random. It is ceremonial. It follows patterns that stretch back to the origin of the human form.

For those who menstruate, this connection is more immediate and visceral. The lunar cycle and the menstrual cycle have long mirrored each other, creating a sacred calendar within the body. But even for those whose blood does not flow monthly, the lunar coding persists. The pull of the moon affects dreams, emotional tides, energetic surges. The body, regardless of gender or reproductive state, remains a lunar instrument. This is not folklore. It is an unspoken biological truth layered with metaphysical implications.

Modern culture has severed this connection. The cycles of work, light, and expectation have flattened time into something linear, mechanical. We are taught to ignore the tides within us, to override them with caffeine, productivity, and numbness. But in doing so, we forfeit something profound. We abandon an ancient intelligence that was never meant to disappear. The moon does not ask to be believed in. It continues its rhythm whether or not we remember. But when we do remember, something lost begins to stir again in the blood.

This stirring is not always comfortable. To feel the moon's pull is to become more sensitive, more attuned. It may bring waves of emotion, sudden fatigue, or heightened clarity. These are not symptoms to suppress. They are signs that the internal compass is realigning. That we are beginning to move not by force, but by flow. And in this flow, power returns. Not the power of dominance, but of deep presence. Of knowing one's timing, one's openings, one's withdrawals.

Many traditions held lunar ceremonies not as rituals of superstition, but as acts of precision. They knew that certain doors only open when the moon is in a particular phase. That certain prayers, certain medicines, certain actions harmonize better when timed to the invisible rhythms of the sky. This was not magical thinking. It was a science of attunement. The kind of science that speaks less in numbers and more in pulses, patterns, and silence. The blood remembers these patterns. Even if the mind forgets, the body does not. And in moments of stillness, especially under moonlight, these memories begin to surface. You may not recall them as thoughts, but as sensations, longings, or sudden insights. These are not coming from outside you. They are coming from within. From the vast archive of lived and inherited memory stored in the blood.

To consciously live in rhythm with the lunar pulse is to begin listening again to the interior landscape. This is not about believing in symbols, but about restoring trust in the sensory intelligence of the body. The moon does not operate in abstractions. Its influence is tangible when we slow down enough to feel it. For many, this begins with observing how energy, mood, and inner voice change across the lunar phases. There are cycles of expansion, release, rest, and illumination. To know them is to stop resisting the body's tides and start moving with them.

The full moon is often misunderstood as a time of chaos, but in truth it is a moment of revelation. What has been hidden beneath the surface becomes visible, emotionally and energetically. For the one who walks a path of awareness, this is a sacred mirror. What arises during this phase is not random. It reflects the deeper waters of the self, the memories stored in the blood, the patterns that have ripened for acknowledgment. These are not to be judged or fixed, but held in clear witnessing. This is the body revealing its own truth under the light of the moon.

The dark moon, often mistaken for absence, holds a different kind of potency. It is the void before the seed, the silence before the word. In this space, the body draws inward. The pulse slows, the psyche descends. This descent is not regression. It is a return to source, a dissolving of identity so that deeper alignment can be reborn. Those who allow themselves to rest during the dark moon often find clarity without effort, guidance without seeking. The blood becomes a still pool in which the next impulse of life can begin to stir.

Ceremonies and rituals aligned with these phases need not be elaborate. What matters is presence. Sitting under the moon with awareness. Breathing into the womb or the belly. Placing a hand over the heart and listening. These are acts of communion, not performance. They open the body to receive what the intellect cannot grasp. The more consistently one aligns with these cycles, the more refined the inner perception becomes. What once felt like intuition begins to reveal itself as remembrance. The body always knew. The moon simply illuminated what had been dormant.

This path is not limited to gender, nor to menstruation. Though the menstrual cycle is a living oracle for many, the lunar blood mystery is not confined to the feminine form. All bodies contain the sacred water, the flowing intelligence of life. The lunar teachings are available to anyone who approaches with humility and devotion. What matters is not biology, but awareness. The one who chooses to align their breath, their rest, their movement, their intention with the rhythms of the moon becomes a vessel for the reweaving of time. Time that flows in spirals, not lines.

In this spiral, blood is not just a carrier of nutrients. It becomes the ink of destiny, the transmitter of memory, the keeper of the soul's agreements. The blood remembers what the mind cannot, and when activated by lunar consciousness, it begins to reveal its secrets. These may arrive in dreams, in sensations, in sudden tears or awakenings. The rational mind may try to explain them away, but the body knows the difference between emotion and initiation. The one who listens begins to walk with a different kind of power. Not loud, not aggressive. But magnetic, clear, and deeply rooted.

To reclaim the moon's secret in the blood is to reclaim your own internal sovereignty. It is to no longer wait for external validation to trust your rhythms. It is to no longer suppress the wave when it rises. It is to allow your healing, your intuition, your knowing, to be guided by the pulse of a greater intelligence that has always been moving through you.

This is not mythology. This is remembrance. And in this remembrance, the body becomes a temple again. A vessel not just of survival, but of sacred timing.

# Releasing the Echoes of Emotional Time

*There is a kind of time that is not measured by clocks. It lives in the tissues, in the breath, in the sudden rush of feeling that seems to come from nowhere. This is emotional time. It does not move forward in a straight line, and it does not obey the intellect. It curls back on itself, looping through moments of impact that were never fully digested. These moments become echoes, still vibrating within the nervous system, still shaping perception, reaction, and belief. They linger not because we are weak or broken, but because the body holds what the mind cannot resolve.*

---

Each emotional imprint leaves a frequency behind. If not felt fully in the moment of its arising, it becomes suspended in the energetic field, waiting. Sometimes it waits for years, for decades. It does not disappear. It becomes the backdrop of identity, coloring the way we see others, the way we relate to love, safety, power. Most of this happens beneath conscious awareness. A person thinks they are responding to the present, when in truth they are reacting to a resonance from the past. The body recognizes something it once knew, and it flinches, contracts, or braces. This is not memory in the mental sense. It is memory stored as pattern, as posture, as tension.

The process of releasing these echoes is not about going back into every painful event and reliving it. It is about creating enough safety in the present to allow the echo to resolve itself. When the body finally feels held, finally feels uninterrupted presence, it begins to soften. What once had to be braced against can be exhaled. This is not a process that responds well to force or urgency. It unfolds at the speed of trust, not willpower. You cannot command the nervous system to unwind. But you can invite it, listen to it, create the conditions for it to return to its natural rhythm.

There is often grief in this unwinding. Grief for the parts of self that had to freeze. Grief for the love that could not be received. Grief for how long it took to understand that emotional time is not weakness, but intelligence. Many have been taught to override their inner cues, to silence their sensitivity, to be functional rather than authentic. The body becomes armored not by choice, but by necessity. That armor eventually becomes heavy. It begins to interfere with joy, with clarity, with connection. And yet even this is not failure. It is a sign that the time for release has arrived.

To walk this path is to recognize that healing is not about becoming someone else. It is about becoming whole again. Not perfect, not untouched, but whole. The echoes of emotional time are not obstacles to this wholeness. They are doorways into it. They point to where life was interrupted, where attention is still needed, where a younger aspect of self is still waiting for resolution. When we meet these places with reverence rather than resistance, something profound shifts. We are no longer trapped in the loop. We are witnessing it from presence, and this witnessing is what allows it to complete.

The nervous system responds to truth, not performance. It can feel the difference between forced affirmation and embodied safety. This is why trying to mentally override an emotional imprint rarely works. The imprint does not live in the rational mind. It lives in the body, in the subconscious, in the layers of sensation and tone that form the inner landscape. Until we learn to speak that language, our deeper layers remain untouched. They may obey externally, but they do not integrate. True release happens only when those inner parts recognize they are finally safe enough to let go.

Safety is not created through avoidance. It is cultivated by turning toward what was once too much. This turning must be gentle, almost like approaching a wild animal in the forest. Too sudden a movement and it flees. But with steady presence, with the absence of threat, even the most guarded places begin to open. The body begins to understand that it no longer lives in the time where the wound was formed. It begins to update its reality.

This is not always linear. The echoes do not surface in an orderly progression. A scent, a word, a glance may pull a hidden memory into the light. Sometimes it feels as if the past is happening all over again, yet this time, there is a witness present. That witness is you. You are no longer the child who endured it. You are the one who can now hold that child in your inner arms. This inner embrace is not symbolic. It is energetic. It is cellular. And it is transformative.

In this work, emotion is not the enemy. It is the teacher. Anger shows where a boundary was crossed. Fear shows where protection was needed. Sadness reveals where love was blocked or lost. Each emotion, when felt cleanly and without judgment, completes its arc. It moves. It passes. It leaves space behind. The danger comes not from the feeling, but from the refusal to feel.

Suppression traps the charge inside the body, where it festers, distorts, and eventually demands expression in unconscious ways.

The echoes can become compulsions, patterns we repeat without knowing why. We are drawn to similar dynamics because the emotional imprint is seeking closure. It is not trying to hurt us. It is trying to heal. But without awareness, we confuse the repetition for fate. We think we are cursed or broken when really, the system is just seeking resolution the only way it knows how. Once we become aware of this, we can begin to offer it a different path. Not reenactment, but release. Not suppression, but presence. Presence is the medicine. It is not passive. It is active, engaged, and deeply attentive. It listens without trying to fix. It holds without collapsing. It feels without drowning. This kind of presence is what the emotional body has always longed for. When it finally arrives, the echoes start to quiet. The loops begin to unwind. The inner storm gives way to stillness, and from that stillness, a new rhythm emerges.

This rhythm is not dictated by fear or reaction. It arises from clarity, from coherence. When the echoes no longer run the show, the self can finally step forward. Not the mask, not the adaptation, but the essence. The real voice. The real longing. The real power. This is what was buried beneath the weight of unprocessed time. It was never gone, only hidden. Releasing the echoes does not diminish you. It reveals you.

To embody this is to walk differently through the world. You begin to feel where others are speaking from their own echoes, and you no longer take it personally. You begin to sense your own patterns before they overtake you, and you meet them with compassion instead of shame. You become fluent in your own inner language, and with this fluency comes a kind of quiet confidence. You no longer need to be ruled by the past, because you have touched the present more deeply than ever before.

And in that present, you find yourself. Not the self that was shaped to survive, but the one that was always meant to live.

# Chapter VI: The Guardian of the Threshold

## The Mask That Blocks the Gate

*There is a face we wear that is not truly ours. It was crafted slowly, layer by layer, as a response to the world's demands and the soul's quiet fear of being seen. This mask does not look like a disguise. It looks like achievement, politeness, competence, spiritual knowledge, or charm. It is built from praise, shaped by punishment, and maintained through habit. We grow so accustomed to it that we begin to believe it is us. But the mask is not the self. It is the barrier that stands at the threshold of the gate.*

---

This gate is not made of stone or wood. It is the subtle doorway through which true transformation must pass. No mask can enter. Only what is raw, unadorned, and real can move beyond it. Yet most spend a lifetime trying to pass through while clutching their carefully constructed identities. The result is spiritual stagnation, or worse, the illusion of progress. The mask becomes more refined, more spiritual, more humble in appearance, but it still obscures the inner light.

The true self does not perform. It does not try to be good, impressive, or enlightened. It simply is. But the mask is terrified of this simplicity. It is built upon the assumption that being raw is not enough, that something must be added, improved, fixed, or controlled. So it seeks perfection, approval, and certainty. It becomes addicted to appearing strong, wise, or unshakable. And in doing so, it resists the very opening that would set it free.

This resistance can be subtle. It might appear as overthinking, self-sabotage, or the endless quest for more knowledge before action is taken. It might show up as chronic busyness, emotional detachment, or the inability to sit still. Beneath these patterns lies a fear that if the mask were dropped, what would be revealed is not beauty, but emptiness. This fear is the gatekeeper. It whispers that your raw self is too much, or not enough. It guards the threshold with shame.

But the irony is that the mask itself is what blocks access to the power it pretends to protect. The more tightly it clings to identity, the more it obscures the flow of life. The body tightens. The breath shortens. The eyes scan instead of see. And the heart, buried beneath the performance, begins to forget its rhythm.

The path through this gate is not about fighting the mask or tearing it off violently. It is about seeing it clearly, naming its shape, and becoming conscious of its function. The moment it is truly seen, it begins to loosen. Its power comes from being mistaken for the self. When that confusion ends, the gate begins to open. Not because the mask was conquered, but because it was understood.

Here, many falter. They confuse the crumbling of the mask with the crumbling of their worth. But you are not what you built to survive. You are what existed before that building began. To remember this is not a metaphor. It is a direct energetic shift. It happens in the body, in the breath, in the space behind the eyes. And when it happens, the air tastes different. Time slows. Something ancient stirs beneath the skin, and you begin to remember the face you had before the world named you.

There is an unmistakable quality to this unveiling. It is not dramatic or loud. It is still, like a breath held at the edge of a dream. What emerges is not a perfected version of the old self, but a presence that no longer needs perfection. There is nothing to manage, prove, or display. The eyes no longer seek confirmation. The body no longer carries the armor of performance. The gate, once sealed by pretense, now opens to the silence that has been waiting beneath all narratives.

This state cannot be forced. It cannot be accessed by adding more techniques, rituals, or identities. It arises through surrender, but not the passive kind. It is a living surrender that requires ferocity and gentleness in equal measure. Ferocity to face the illusions that fed the mask. Gentleness to hold what trembles underneath. These two forces, when harmonized, dissolve the false separation between the sacred and the ordinary. Life is no longer divided. Every act, however small, becomes an initiation.

The challenge is not the lack of access to this state. It is its unbearable clarity. Once the gate opens, what was once tolerable becomes intolerable. The lies we told ourselves no longer fit. The relationships built on mutual masking begin to crack. Work that served the mask begins to feel hollow. This is where many turn back. They mistake the disorientation for failure. But it is not failure. It is the body, mind, and soul adjusting to the absence of false structure.

What replaces the mask is not another role. It is a capacity to be nothing and everything in a single breath. To speak only when the voice is rooted in truth. To walk without needing to be seen. To love without collapsing into the need to be loved in return. This is not the end of struggle. But the struggle shifts. It becomes a creative tension rather than a survival reflex. And in that tension, the soul becomes audible again.

The intelligence that flows once the gate is passed does not speak in language alone. It speaks in sensation, symbol, synchronicity, and silence. It guides from within, not with promises or praise, but with a clarity that cuts through confusion without violence. It is not interested in your success as the world defines it. It is only interested in your alignment with what is real. The closer you stay to that alignment, the lighter the path becomes, even when it passes through shadow.

The true face is not a static essence. It is not an idea or ideal self. It is a living presence that shapeshifts with truth. It may look like strength or softness, clarity or mystery, stillness or fire. It cannot be pinned down. And it cannot be fully seen in the mirror of the world, because the world often reflects the mask, not the self. The only mirror that reveals the real face is the one held in the stillness of the heart.

To live beyond the mask is to live as a threshold. You become a gate through which others glimpse their own light. Not because you teach or preach, but because you no longer block the current of being. You move with it. You let it speak through your eyes, your hands, your silences. The gate you passed becomes a door you hold open. And the mask, once so carefully worn, becomes unnecessary. Not discarded in rebellion, but laid down in peace, like a tool no longer needed, because the work has become you.

# Naming the Unseen Fear

*There is a fear that does not speak in words. It hides beneath the surface of ordinary thoughts, beneath even the emotions we allow ourselves to feel. This fear is not loud. It does not shout in panic or tremble in obvious distress. It lives in silence, wrapped in forgetfulness, disguised by certainty or distraction. And because it is unseen, it governs more than we realize. It shapes choices, draws boundaries, and limits expansion while wearing the mask of logic, caution, or even wisdom.*

---

To begin to name this fear is not a matter of simply identifying an emotion. It requires a deeper act: the willingness to sit in a space where language dissolves and where what has been hidden for decades begins to stir. The unseen fear is ancient. It is often not even ours alone. It is passed through bloodlines, stories, and collective patterns. It becomes encoded in the body, felt as resistance in the chest, tension in the jaw, or a subtle shrinking back from possibility.

The mind is clever in defending itself from such exposure. It will create justifications, redirections, spiritual rationalizations, and even noble ideals to avoid confronting what lies underneath. But no real transformation can occur while this fear remains unnamed. Until it is brought into the field of awareness, it will continue to guide actions from the shadows. Its greatest power is not in what it causes, but in how it avoids being seen.

There is often an assumption that what we fear most is failure, rejection, abandonment, or death. These are real, but they are often masks for something more primal: the fear of dissolving. Not physical death, but the crumbling of the false self. The ego senses this and tightens its grip, whispering that to let go would be annihilation. It is here that most turn away, retreating into familiarity, even if that familiarity is suffering. The unknown becomes more terrifying than the known pain.

To name the unseen fear is to admit that we are not in control of as much as we believed. It is to see that much of what we thought we wanted was shaped by avoidance, by the hunger to never feel that one thing again. The thing we never talk about. The moment that broke our sense of safety. The silence after a betrayal. The loneliness no one witnessed. These unspoken experiences become the architecture of the fear that moves through our lives.

And yet, when we bring presence to this fear, something unexpected begins to happen. It begins to shift. Not because we conquer it, but because we stop turning away from it. The act of naming is not about labeling or intellectualizing. It is about witnessing. When we say, "I feel the fear of disappearing," or "I sense a terror of being fully seen," or "I fear that my power will destroy what I love," we are not making declarations. We are making space for the real.

At first, this naming may come in whispers. It might feel awkward or incomplete. The fear may resist even being looked at directly. It may appear as numbness or confusion. But even this is a sign of movement. The unseen fear thrives in disconnection. The moment we bring warm attention to it, even without full understanding, it begins to soften. The nervous system responds to presence. The body, once frozen around a wound, begins to thaw. The pattern starts to loosen.

In that softening, we may begin to hear the stories the body has held in silence. Not in words, but in impressions, fragments, memories, or sensations that were too overwhelming at the time to be processed. These impressions were stored away, locked behind tension and guarded by survival. Now, through presence, they surface not to destabilize us, but to be seen, held, and finally released.

The fear is not trying to hurt us. It is not our enemy. It is a loyal force that once protected the inner child, the vulnerable self, the one who did not yet know how to stand in the fire without being consumed. But we are not that child anymore. We have access now to awareness, to breath, to grounded stillness. And from this place, we can hold what once would have broken us.

Often, the fear speaks in the language of contraction. The body tightens, the heart races, the breath shortens. In this moment, the old imprint is alive. It is not a concept. It is a lived experience returning. If we try to talk ourselves out of it or rush to solve it, we miss the invitation. The way through is stillness. It is breath, not explanation. It is sitting with the fear without needing to fix or flee. This is not inaction. It is deep engagement with the energy beneath the surface.

What begins to emerge through this process is clarity. Not the clarity of intellectual understanding, but the kind that comes from a quiet internal knowing. We begin to see the choices that were not truly ours. We notice where we have been performing safety rather than living authenticity. We realize how much energy has been spent avoiding a feeling that was never as dangerous as we believed. And with this realization, we begin to reclaim our power.

Naming the fear is not a one-time event. It is a practice. Each time we meet a new edge, a new threshold of expansion, the fear may rise again, asking if we are ready to move without being ruled by it. This is not failure. It is the nature of growth. The spiral returns us to the same place, but with new eyes. We are not who we were the last time we stood here.

As the layers peel away, we may discover that some fears were never personal. They were inherited, absorbed from collective fields, or encoded through ancestral lines. This recognition is not an excuse to disown them, but a deeper invitation to be the one who transforms them. Not by force, but by becoming the still point where the echo stops repeating.

From this stillness, we can choose differently. We can speak the words that were once swallowed. We can show up with openness where we once closed. We can risk being seen, heard, felt. And in that risk, we become more real. Not because the fear has vanished, but because it no longer decides who we are allowed to be.

There is great humility in this process. We learn to listen to the subtle, to track the quiet movements beneath the surface. We begin to notice the spaces where fear tries to hide behind control or ambition. And instead of reacting, we pause. We breathe. We ask, "What is truly needed here?" This simple question dismantles the illusion. It brings the unconscious into awareness, not as an idea, but as a felt truth.

Naming the unseen fear returns us to choice. It gives us back the capacity to act from clarity rather than compulsion. It invites us to walk forward not because we are certain, but because we are present. And that presence, that willingness to stay open in the midst of uncertainty, is the true mark of power.

This is the gateway. This is the quiet revolution that transforms everything.

## Passing Through by Standing Still

*There is a paradox embedded in every true path of transformation: the gateway opens not through striving, but through stillness. Not by pushing harder, but by pausing deeper. We are conditioned to believe that forward motion is the only direction of growth, that evolution demands effort, speed, and constant doing. But the deeper laws are older than motion. They are inscribed in silence, in still water, in breath held at the moment between inhale and exhale.*

---

To pass through the thresholds that matter, we must learn the forgotten art of standing still. Not stillness as inertia or avoidance, but as precise alignment with what is present. A stillness that listens more deeply than the surface mind can comprehend. One that holds awareness in the body, in sensation, in the subtle rhythms beneath thought.

Standing still is not passive. It is not about stopping life. It is about stopping the illusion that we must chase, fix, or force our way into the next phase. It is about refusing the panic that tells us we must move just to escape what is here. This kind of stillness is an act of sacred defiance. It says, "I will not abandon the moment. I will not abandon myself."

In this stillness, time behaves differently. What once felt like stagnation becomes revelation. Layers that could not be accessed in motion begin to rise. Old stories, old survival patterns, begin to loosen. The nervous system, given permission to rest, reveals what it has been holding for years. And when we are not running, these patterns cannot hide. We see the shape of our inner architecture. We see where we collapse and where we brace. We see the doorway we never noticed because we were moving too fast.

To stand still is to surrender the need to perform transformation. It means not needing to have the right words or the perfect insight. It means meeting what is raw, what is unresolved, what is still aching — and not turning away. This level of presence is its own kind of movement. It is the movement of consciousness settling into truth. It is the movement of energy realigning itself because space has finally been made.

This process is not romantic. It does not feel like victory. It often feels like undoing, like being stripped bare. Because in stillness, there is nothing to distract us from ourselves. There is no task to prove our worth, no goal to justify our identity. There is only what is. This is where the deeper passage happens. When we stop pushing, the real journey begins.

Some initiations cannot be accelerated. Some gates will not open until we are able to be fully still before them. Not because the gate is punishing us, but because its vibration will not respond to force. It responds to resonance. And we cannot force resonance. We must become it. We must become quiet enough to feel the subtle pulse that tells us where we are holding too tightly and where we are not yet fully here.

In this way, standing still becomes a mirror. It shows us what we have tried to bypass. It reflects the pain we thought we had resolved but only buried. It reveals the inner clenching that creates distortion in everything we touch. And as we see it clearly, without judgment, without panic, we begin to dissolve the interference.

Standing still also teaches trust. Not blind faith, but embodied trust in the intelligence of timing. It reveals that life is not linear. That depth does not unfold on command. That there is a wisdom beneath appearances that is guiding us whether or not we understand. This is not something the mind can grasp. It is something the body begins to feel when it is no longer rushing to become something else.

When the body no longer rushes to become, something ancient is restored. The rhythm of nature begins to emerge from within. You begin to sense the slow intelligence of roots, of tides, of breath itself. Movement becomes a response, not a reaction. Instead of reaching, you begin to receive. Instead of efforting your way toward the next step, you notice that the next step is already forming beneath your feet.

This is the paradox that few are willing to live long enough to experience. Stillness, sustained without resistance, generates motion of another order. Not the motion of physical momentum or external progression, but the subtle current of alignment. It is this current that carries the soul across thresholds the ego could never force open. It is this current that repositions you into experiences your mind could not have orchestrated.

Those who dwell in this kind of presence begin to emit a frequency that alters the space around them. Not because they are trying to, but because they have ceased distorting the field with noise. Their stillness becomes a kind of gravity. Others feel it, though they may not understand it. It is the presence of someone who no longer leaks energy through grasping.

Someone who no longer fractures their essence to fit expectations. Someone who no longer apologizes for being here.

To pass through by standing still is to meet the threshold as an equal. Not as someone pleading for access, but as someone who has become ready. This readiness is not born of preparation in the usual sense. It is born of the willingness to feel, to stay, to not flinch. The gate opens not because you have earned it, but because you have stopped pretending. You are no longer elsewhere. You are exactly where the opening is.

The soul does not require theatrics to grow. It requires honesty. It requires space. It requires a nervous system that is not constantly bracing against itself. Stillness allows these conditions to form. And when they do, what once seemed unreachable begins to move toward you. Not because you chased it, but because you tuned yourself to its signal. This is why the sages spoke so often of receptivity, of surrender, of waiting without passivity. They were not preaching inaction. They were describing the gateway between timelines.

Most people live their entire lives in exile from this inner stillness. Not because it is hidden, but because it is too quiet for the distracted self to notice. They prefer movement because it masks the ache. They prefer answers because they fear the silence. But those who have tasted the clarity that only stillness brings know that there is no replacement for its depth. No shortcut around the surrender it requires.

In this stillness, your true coordinates are revealed. You see what is yours and what is not. You begin to withdraw energy from battles that were never yours to fight. You start to notice how often you were moving out of fear rather than alignment. And slowly, your decisions start to reflect a different center. One not driven by urgency, but by resonance. Not dictated by the world's clock, but by a deeper rhythm that does not rush.

To cultivate this way of being is to remember your original tempo. The one that was never fragmented by expectation. The one that did not require justification to exist. It is a slow return, not to who you were, but to what you are beneath all the motion. And once you arrive, you will see that you never needed to escape the moment. You only needed to fully enter it.

This is the movement that changes everything: the shift from doing to being, from striving to allowing, from reaching to remembering. It is here, in the stillness you once avoided, that the hidden gate begins to glow. And without forcing anything, you pass through.

# Chapter VII: The Seed That Contains the Star

**The Code Hidden in the Core**

*There is something buried so deep within you that it has never been touched by fear, time, or distortion. It does not speak loudly. It does not seek attention. It simply is—a silent, living intelligence coiled in the center of your being, untouched by external noise. Most pass their lives orbiting around it, unaware that everything they seek is already encoded in the core they avoid.*

---

This core is not a metaphor. It is a living frequency field, vibrating with the memory of your unbroken self. It carries patterns older than language, signals that pulse through your biology and psyche, even when you are unaware of their presence. In ancient systems, this was often called the *divine spark*, the *sacred flame*, the *seed of origin*. It is the blueprint that remains whole no matter what experiences fracture the outer self.

But why is it hidden? Why do we so easily forget its presence?

Because the outer world trains us to build from the outside in. From achievements, titles, beliefs, and personas. We are encouraged to layer ourselves in borrowed structures, to conform to the forms that win approval. Slowly, the inner voice becomes faint, buried beneath the noise of becoming what others understand. But the code never leaves. It simply waits.

This code is not something you must earn access to. It's not a prize for the enlightened. It is the truest structure of your being, embedded in your physical and energetic anatomy. It is the rhythm beneath your pulse, the geometry behind your instincts, the pattern that recurs in your choices when you are fully aligned. You've glimpsed it in moments when everything felt clear for no reason, when you acted without hesitation and everything clicked into place. Those were moments when the core was speaking through you.

The challenge is not to create this code, but to recover the clarity to read it. To listen without interfering. To sit still long enough to feel what's already written into your breath, your gut, your silence. This clarity cannot be rushed. It requires you to step out of the noise long enough for the deeper current to rise.

Many try to force alignment by mimicking others who appear to have found their path. But no path built on imitation can awaken the code within. What awakens it is honesty. The kind of honesty that strips you bare—not in front of others, but in front of yourself. When you stop trying to be impressive, or spiritual, or even healed, the signal begins to strengthen. Because the code does not respond to performance. It responds to presence.

You can think of this code as a silent compass that never points toward safety or applause, but always toward truth. That is why following it often feels dangerous to the ego. It will lead you away from what is familiar, even if what is familiar has brought you comfort. It does not negotiate with your attachments. It pulls you toward coherence, even if that coherence costs you your persona. And this is where many resist.

But those who listen, who dare to trust the inner signals more than the outer narratives, begin to notice something strange. Doors open that logic cannot explain. Encounters occur with eerie precision. Insights arrive that feel both ancient and immediate. The world responds to the one who moves from core.

The code does not speak in language but in impulse. It moves through sensation, intuition, and the subtle architecture of resonance. When something feels deeply right without justification, when your body relaxes before your mind understands why, the code is in motion. It is not dramatic. It is exact. It recalibrates your path not by shouting but by subtly realigning what no longer fits. Those who learn to listen find themselves stepping into spaces they did not plan for but somehow always belonged to.

To live from the core is to submit to a different intelligence—one that does not prioritize safety, but clarity. It may lead you to exit what once defined you. It may require you to say no to offers that flatter your persona but would fracture your integrity. It may reveal that the cost of belonging to others was the abandonment of yourself. These revelations are not punishments. They are invitations to return to alignment.

This is why the process is rarely convenient. The code will dissolve false timelines. It will unmask relationships built on performance. It will pull you out of anything that keeps you pretending. And while this may feel like loss, it is only the clearing of distortion. You cannot hear the instruction of the core while feeding what is false. The two cannot coexist.

Those who resist this unraveling usually do so not because they doubt the truth, but because they fear its consequence. They sense that their current world is held together by compromises. If the core is truly followed, that world must fall. And yet, what comes after is not destruction but restoration. What remains after the purge is what was always real. What arrives after the silence is what was always yours.

Some wait for certainty before they act. They want guarantees before surrendering. But the code never offers certainty in the way the mind demands it. It speaks through a deeper kind of knowing, one that does not come with proof but with peace. The more you test this peace, the more reliable it becomes. Over time, it teaches you to trust not through belief, but through direct experience.

There is no map to this process, but there are signs. You will begin to feel more real, even if nothing outside you has changed. Your voice will carry a different weight, not because it is louder, but because it is rooted. You will stop chasing things that once felt urgent. Not from apathy, but because your desire has been purified. You no longer want what is not meant for you. This is not detachment. It is clarity.

From this place, manifestation shifts. It no longer arises from desperation or compensation. It becomes a byproduct of alignment. What you create carries the signature of your essence. What you attract arrives through resonance, not strategy. You no longer manipulate outcomes. You shape reality by being congruent with what is already true.

The core does not demand perfection. It requires presence. You will still forget, still fall into patterns, still meet your shadows. But now, you return faster. Now, you know where home is. And even when you are off-course, the pulse of the code continues to beat beneath the noise, always waiting for your attention, always ready to guide you back.

To live this way is not to escape the world, but to meet it without distortion. It is to stand at the center of yourself and act from what cannot be shaken. This is not power in the way the world defines it. It is not dominance or control. It is coherence. It is the quiet authority of one who has remembered who they are.

And once you begin to live from that remembering, you do not go back. Because once the code is felt in its fullness, nothing less will satisfy.

## Death as Fertile Ground

*There is a death that does not end life, but begins it.*

---

Most fear death because they misunderstand what it asks of them. They imagine it only as a final severing, a black void, the closing of the story. But in the symbolic traditions that hold the deepest truths, death is the gate through which all transformation walks. Nothing becomes sacred until it has died in some form. The seed does not sprout unless it breaks. The identity does not evolve unless it dissolves. The soul does not remember unless the self forgets what it thought it was.

This is not metaphor. It is law. In every tradition where sacred initiation was real, the initiate had to die before they could carry the light. Not physically, but internally. Their former self—composed of fear, expectation, and illusion—had to be stripped away, sometimes violently. They were buried before they were crowned. They were broken before they were aligned. Death, in this context, is not an end. It is a preparation.

And yet, most of the world is structured to avoid this death. People cling to roles, identities, beliefs, and comfort zones with the desperation of someone afraid to disappear. But what they protect is the very shell that suffocates them. What they refuse to let die is what keeps them from being reborn. They mourn the idea of loss without realizing that their rebirth has been waiting behind it all along.

True death comes uninvited. It is not planned. It does not fit on a calendar. It arrives in the form of endings, betrayals, losses, breakdowns. But these moments are not punishments. They are sacred interventions. They strip away what is untrue so that what is essential can finally surface. The ego interprets it as collapse, but the soul recognizes it as reconfiguration.

If you are in a season where everything feels like it is falling apart, you are not failing. You are in the soil. This is the moment where the seed begins its silent conversation with the dark. It is not yet time to rise, but it is time to listen. Because in this death, a new design is forming. The old codes are being rewritten. And the identity you once curated so carefully is being returned to dust, not as destruction, but as nourishment for something far more real.

Letting the old self die is not a passive act. It is not numb surrender. It is sacred participation. You watch the stories fall away. You let the masks rot in your hands. You say goodbye to voices that used to define you. And in doing so, you begin to remember the one who was there before the performance began. The one who never needed validation to exist. The one who knows how to listen when all else has gone quiet.

Many try to bypass this phase. They want light without descent. They want truth without fracture. But anything that is truly holy must pass through the fire. It must be purified, emptied, reshaped. This is not cruelty. It is initiation. What cannot survive the fire was never real to begin with.

There is a humility that arises when you let yourself die in this way. You stop pretending to be in control. You stop seeking applause. You stop negotiating with life. And in that stripped-down silence, a new kind of presence awakens—one that does not rely on outcome or identity. It simply is. Whole. Rooted. Ready.

The soil of death is not barren. It is dense with the nutrients of what has been. It holds memory, wisdom, fragments of past selves. And what rises from it is not a replacement, but a refinement.

From this refinement, a truer architecture of self begins to emerge. Not one crafted by survival or shaped by the gaze of others, but one that rises from deep alignment with the essence beneath all names. This emergence does not happen all at once. It is subtle, sometimes imperceptible. You notice that your old reactions no longer take hold. You begin to speak less from defense and more from clarity. Your decisions are no longer fueled by fear of losing what never truly belonged to you. The voice within becomes steadier, not louder, as if it finally trusts that you are listening.

This is how the cycle of inner death becomes the root of embodied life. It teaches you not just how to shed, but how to inhabit what is real. It teaches you that rebirth is not something that happens later, once the grief is done, but something that begins in the very moment you allow yourself to meet the grief without resistance. That single breath of honest surrender marks the turning point. It does not remove the ache, but it alters the relationship to it. You stop trying to push it away or dress it up in meaning. You begin to understand that the ache is the echo of something sacred returning.

There is a kind of courage that matures in the heart when you stop fearing death in all its forms. You become less interested in appearances and more attuned to essence. You stop clinging to the illusion of stability and begin to trust in the fluidity of the unknown. The mind may still panic, still want to anchor itself in fixed narratives, but the soul has tasted something deeper, and it no longer consents to being reduced.

When you walk through the terrain of inner death consciously, you develop eyes that see beneath the surface of things. You begin to recognize others who have walked the same path. There is a subtle weight to them, not heavy, but grounded. They do not rush to give answers or speak over silence. They carry something ancient in their presence, a quality shaped by descent and tempered by fire. They are not interested in convincing or converting. They are simply rooted, and in that rootedness, they transmit.

This is the power of dying well. It does not only change the one who passes through the threshold. It creates a field. A kind of signal that resonates beyond the individual. Your descent becomes a map for others, not through instruction, but through transmission. You become proof that dissolution is not the end. That something stable and luminous exists beyond the masks and roles. That the soul can be known, not as a concept, but as a living current.

The modern world offers few rituals for death that is not physical. There is no ceremonial space for shedding a former self. No sacred acknowledgment of internal endings. But this is where your own awareness becomes the altar. You do not need an audience to mark the transformation. You need only honesty, stillness, and the willingness to let something go without knowing what will take its place.

That unknowing is the final veil. It is where all the mental scaffolding begins to fall. You stand at the threshold without certainty, without plan, and you allow yourself to be re-formed by what you cannot yet name. This is where the false self gives way to the initiated self. Not the perfected one, but the one who knows how to walk forward while carrying emptiness with reverence.

The world does not need more people who know how to win. It needs more who know how to let go. More who are not afraid of the dark because they have walked through it. More who have been hollowed out enough to be filled with something real. That is the fertile ground. That is where resurrection becomes not a story, but a rhythm.

Let what is ready to die in you die completely. Not because you are broken, but because you are becoming. Let the ashes speak. Let them bless the soil. And when something begins to rise from within, do not rush to label it. Let it breathe. Let it become. Let it remind you that everything sacred was once buried. And that what blooms after death carries the weight of truth.

# Becoming That Which You Already Are

*There is no real becoming without remembering.*

---

The journey of spiritual maturation is not about constructing a self, but about uncovering the essence that has never been lost, only obscured. This is the paradox that both humbles and empowers. What you seek is not ahead of you in time, but beneath the layers of illusion that time has wrapped around your being. To become who you truly are, you must begin to unlearn who you were told to be.

You were not born as a blank slate. You arrived encoded, carrying imprints from soul-lineage, ancestral memory, and cosmic intention. Before you were shaped by family, language, and culture, there was already a unique frequency etched into your being. This frequency is not a concept to be grasped, but a living presence to be attuned to. It is not accessed through striving or imitation. It reveals itself in the stillness that remains after you stop trying to be anything.

Most systems of conditioning begin with the premise that you are incomplete. That you must add knowledge, discipline, status, or enlightenment in order to become whole. This keeps the seeker in perpetual deferral, always reaching, always measuring, always preparing. But what if the work is not to become more, but to remove what is false? What if the most radical transformation is not forward motion, but a return to what has always been quietly waiting within?

The ancient traditions knew this. Initiation was not about improvement. It was about piercing through the veil of appearances to remember the self beneath the mask. The rites were designed not to build a better ego, but to dissolve the false identity that shields the soul. Only then could the hidden pattern emerge. Only then could the initiate take their rightful place as one who walks between the worlds, not because they had mastered something external, but because they had surrendered everything that was not essential.

To walk this path is to stop seeking externally what you already carry internally. It is to shift the entire axis of attention from projection to presence. You are not a problem to be fixed. You are a mystery to be revealed. And that revelation requires not perfection, but permission.

Permission to be real. To be quiet. To be messy and luminous in the same breath.

As long as you identify with the persona constructed for survival, you will remain in exile from your deeper knowing. The persona is not evil. It is simply insufficient. It was built to navigate a world of contracts and expectations. But the soul does not operate on those terms. It speaks in sensation, symbol, and resonance. It moves in spirals, not straight lines. It does not demand performance. It requires presence.

There comes a moment on the inner path when the scaffolding begins to shake. The titles, the beliefs, even the spiritual identities start to feel heavy. What once gave meaning now feels brittle. This is not a crisis. It is a signal. You are nearing the threshold. The deeper self is rising, and it is incompatible with the costume. The closer you get to essence, the less you can pretend.

This shedding is often mistaken for loss. But what falls away was never truly you. It was a collection of adaptations, a carefully curated echo of belonging. As it dissolves, grief may arise—not because your truth is dying, but because you spent so long living as someone you never truly were. That grief is holy. It is the mourning of a life unlived. It clears space for something more honest to emerge.

What emerges from the ashes of that false self is not another identity to wear, but a presence that does not need to be named. It does not rely on validation or reflection. It simply *is*, and in that is-ness, there is an unshakable peace. The mind may not know how to define it, and that is precisely the point. What is true at the level of essence cannot be contained by the tools of language. It can only be known through direct experience.

To become what you already are is to stop fragmenting your attention. Most people live in pieces—part of them performing, part of them suppressing, part of them observing, and only a small sliver actually *inhabiting*. This inner fragmentation creates a subtle exhaustion, a tension that can never fully resolve. But when you allow all parts of you to return to the same center, something clicks into alignment. You begin to function as a whole being, not as a collection of roles.

This alignment is not static. It breathes with you. It shifts, recalibrates, and deepens with every layer of truth you are willing to embody. But it always begins with presence. And presence begins with stillness. Not necessarily the absence of movement, but the absence of pretending. The absence of running. In that stillness, the quiet self begins to speak. Not with urgency, but with clarity.

You may discover that what you feared to be your flaws are simply misdirected powers. What looked like weakness was just a gift in exile. The part of you that feels too sensitive, too intense, too strange, is often the exact frequency you came to embody on behalf of the whole. The work is not to dull it or mask it, but to refine your relationship with it. To listen. To understand its origin. To offer it a home in your awareness so that it can serve its true purpose.

As you move deeper into this embodiment, you will notice a shift in how you relate to time. The future loses its pull. The past loses its grip. What matters is not what might happen or what already happened, but how fully you are rooted in what is happening *now*. From this root, a new kind of intelligence emerges—not the intellect of control, but the wisdom of responsiveness. Life begins to organize itself around your coherence.

This is the state from which true creation flows. Not from effort or ambition, but from resonance. You no longer manifest by trying to manipulate outcomes, but by aligning so completely with your essence that life has no choice but to mirror that alignment. The universe does not respond to your words. It responds to your frequency. And the most potent frequency is authenticity.

There is no formula for this path. There is only devotion. Not to a system or ideology, but to truth itself. To living in a way that refuses to betray the soul. Every time you choose presence over performance, alignment over approval, silence over noise, you come closer to the source that animates your being. You strip away the costume and find, underneath it, a self that was never waiting to be created. Only remembered.

Becoming that which you already are is not a grand event. It is a thousand quiet choices made in the intimacy of your own awareness. It is a willingness to be faithful to your inner knowing, even when it makes no sense to the outside world. Especially then. For the deeper self does not seek permission. It only seeks your return.

This is not the end of your path. It is the return to the place you never left. Not as the child who arrived in innocence, but as the one who has walked through the forgetting and chosen, again and again, to remember. Not with the mind, but with the whole of your being.

The essence was never gone. Only hidden. And now, unveiled, it moves not in search of identity, but as a quiet fire that knows exactly what it is.

# VOLUME II

The Temple and the Return

# Introduction

*There comes a moment on the inner path when the longing shifts. At first, the seeker moves outward, reaching for knowledge, teachers, symbols, and signs. But eventually, something quiet and undeniable begins to emerge from within. It is not a new desire, but the return of a very old one. It has no name, yet it draws you with precision. It is not ambition. It is not curiosity. It is the call home.*

---

This part of the journey does not offer grand revelations or cosmic shortcuts. Instead, it invites you into something far more intimate: the reentry into your own sacred structure. The temple was never a place outside of you. It was always within, waiting for your return. Not a return to who you were before the world shaped you, but a return to the unshaped presence beneath every role you've ever played.
The temple is the body, but not only the physical body. It is the emotional terrain, the energetic architecture, the ancient intelligence that remembers what your conscious mind has forgotten. And just as ancient temples were aligned with cosmic grids and star paths, your inner temple has a design—subtle, but precise. You were not born into randomness. You are the echo of a geometry that speaks in stillness, in symbols, in the unspoken knowing that comes not from books, but from deep contact with yourself.
This section is not about improvement. It is about remembrance. Each chapter acts like a tuning fork, awakening the memory stored in the marrow, the breath, the pulse. You are not being asked to add anything. You are being invited to remove what never truly belonged, to dissolve the masks that once protected you but now obscure your vision.
Here, the process is not linear. It is cyclical, rhythmic, and lunar. It speaks in the language of tides, of dreams, of deep listening. You may find yourself pulled backward as much as forward. That is not regression—it is the necessary spiral of descent and ascent, of confronting what was hidden to recover what is true. The return is not a straight line. It is a sacred spiral that brings you deeper into yourself with each revolution.

You will touch grief that does not belong only to you. You will feel joy that comes not from circumstance but from presence. You will encounter resistance, shame, and tenderness, not as blocks, but as guardians at the gate. The threshold is not something to cross quickly. It is something to *become*. When you learn to sit in that threshold without rushing through it, you are no longer trying to escape your humanity. You are sanctifying it.

The temple and the return are not concepts to be understood. They are experiences to be entered. In this part of the book, allow yourself to walk not with the mind, but with the body, the breath, and the intuition that knows how to read what has no words. Let each page be a step further into the quiet center of your own knowing. Let it bring you to the place where the sacred is no longer something to reach for—but something that lives, fully, where you are.

# The Return Is Not Repetition

*There is a quiet misconception that often takes root in the seeker's mind: that growth is linear, that transformation should keep us moving forward in ever-expanding strides, and that the return—when it comes—should resemble a triumphant homecoming without shadows. But the true return does not move along the clean axis of time. It spirals. It loops. It turns us around not to disorient, but to reveal.*

---

The soul does not measure progress as the mind does. What feels like circling back to the same lesson is often the opportunity to meet it at a deeper octave. The repetition is not in the experience, but in our perception of it. If the same fear, the same wound, or the same relationship pattern appears again, it is not always a sign of failure. It may be the soul returning to the exact point where the fracture first occurred—not to repeat the injury, but to rewrite its meaning.

In the sacred traditions, the return is not viewed as going backward. It is seen as the reintegration of the fragmented self. It is the reweaving of the thread that was cut, forgotten, or denied. This return demands presence, not performance. It asks for sincerity, not speed. And it will often arrive wearing the face of the past—not to imprison us, but to offer us the keys to what we once could not face.

To return consciously is to walk into the same room with new eyes. You do not pretend the room has changed. You see more of what was always there. That awareness is what alters everything. You may return to the same landscape, the same body, the same silence, but if your perception has ripened, the experience is no longer the same. You are not the same.

Some resist the return because it carries the taste of regression. But true regression is only possible when we turn away from the lesson altogether. If we stay, if we breathe through it, if we dare to face the discomfort it brings, the return becomes alchemy. The very ground that once collapsed beneath you becomes the foundation you now stand on with clarity and strength.

The ego seeks novelty. It wants to move on, to avoid being seen as stuck or repetitive. But the soul is not concerned with appearances. It moves through rhythm, through the deeper pulse of transformation that is not always visible to the outside world. There may be no applause for facing the same wound for the fifth or tenth time, but each time you do so with more softness, more presence, more truth, you are dissolving the illusion that held you captive.

The return, then, is not a duplication of the past. It is a re-entry into a moment with greater wholeness. Where you once arrived fragmented, you now bring coherence. Where you once carried defense, you now bring openness. It is not about fixing what was broken. It is about allowing what was left behind to finally be received.

The spiral teaches this. It brings us back to the same point on the circle, but always from a slightly higher place. In sacred geometry, the spiral is not a closed loop, but an ever-expanding pattern of ascent. It turns inward only to carry us further outward. This movement is subtle. It requires trust. And it will rarely feel like progress in the ways we are taught to measure it.

You may stand in the same temple, face the same silence, and kneel at the same threshold. But this time, something in you is more available. You are not reenacting. You are remembering. And in that remembering, a deeper truth is made visible, one that could not be accessed before.

The spiral return is not soft because life wants to be gentle. It is soft because you are no longer fighting it. The energy that was once spent resisting is now available to perceive. What you thought was an obstacle becomes an oracle. And what you once ran from becomes a sacred mirror reflecting the self you were too afraid to meet.

There is a moment in every cycle when you realize that nothing has changed, and yet everything has changed. The faces may be familiar, the patterns recognizable, but you are no longer orbiting from survival. You are witnessing from presence. Even pain, when held this way, begins to reveal its intelligence. The wound that once silenced you may now open into a voice, a truth, or a vision that needed the space of time to be fully born.

If you listen closely, you will notice that the terrain of return is not made of repeated days. It is made of layered depth. One sorrow speaks to another. One joy recalls an earlier one. The inner architecture begins to resemble a mandala, not a path with a finish line. And this shift from the linear to the spiral marks a key transformation: you stop trying to arrive, and instead begin to embody.

This is not a resignation. It is not a giving up. It is a turning toward. A recognition that growth is not only forward movement but fuller presence. That maturity is not marked by distance from your old self, but by your ability to meet that self with wisdom and compassion. What you thought you needed to forget or outgrow becomes part of the very soil that holds you now.

When initiates were trained in ancient rites, they were often led in circles intentionally. It was never a mistake. The disorientation was part of the decoding. By confronting the same symbol, the same threshold, the same story from different angles, a deeper layer would reveal itself. They learned to stop asking, "Why am I here again?" and instead began to ask, "What am I now able to see?"

Your own return will likely not come in ceremonial robes. It may look like a familiar heartbreak. An old fear. A repeated silence. But if you meet it with the eyes of the soul, it becomes sacred material. And if you stay long enough in its presence, it will offer something it could not before.

This is the paradox of the spiral: it mimics repetition only to dismantle it. What you think is recurring is, in truth, completing. But the completion is not in escape. It is in full contact. You break the loop not by rejecting it, but by becoming conscious inside it. You become the still point within the turning.

Eventually, the return becomes recognition. You no longer fear the old places. You no longer collapse into old narratives. You greet them as teachers, not tests. And in doing so, you reclaim the energy once tied up in resistance. You do not avoid your story. You rewrite it in real time, by standing fully inside it, awake.

The return, then, is a portal. It does not deliver you to the past. It delivers the past to your present awareness, asking only that you see it clearly, hold it honestly, and walk through it with integrity. You are not the same one who left. You are the one who now knows what the journey was really for. And so, when you meet that old pattern, that familiar face, that inner child waiting still at the threshold, do not turn away. Step into the spiral. Let the moment turn through you. Let it complete what it began. Let it show you that you were never circling in vain. You were spiraling toward yourself.

## The Seed Remembers the Tree

*There is an ancient knowing carried in the silence of a seed. Long before it touches soil, it holds the shape of the tree it will become. Not just its physical form, but its essence. The way it will bend toward light. The taste of its fruit. The stretch of its roots through darkness. It is not a blank beginning, but a concentrated memory. A code encoded in stillness, waiting for the right conditions to unfurl.*

---

This is not metaphor. It is pattern. All living things carry the echo of their future within their origin. Not as a rigid script, but as a field of possibility shaped by essence. The seed is not instructed from the outside. It is awakened from within. And this awakening happens not through instruction, but through contact. With earth. With water. With gravity. With time.

You too carry a code.

Not the kind dictated by culture or circumstance, but one that exists beneath them. A deep remembering that cannot be taught, only revealed. You may have spent years looking outward for guidance, searching books, mentors, teachings, rituals. And while each of these may offer something, none of them can substitute for the precise intelligence already seeded within you. That intelligence speaks in sensation. In dreams. In the pull toward what feels right even when it is inexplicable. It is the soul's orientation, not the ego's ambition.

When we speak of returning to your essence, we are not asking you to become something new. We are inviting you to become what has always been there, hidden beneath layers of survival, adaptation, and forgetfulness. The seed never forgets. It simply waits.

This waiting is not passive. It is sacred timing. The seed does not rush. It does not force growth when the frost still clings to the soil. It does not perform maturity to meet expectations. It knows that rushing would only deform what it is meant to become. And so it stays inward until the conditions match the call. Until life becomes invitation rather than demand. In the human journey, this often looks like dormancy. Periods where nothing seems to be happening, when no clarity arrives, when action feels impossible. But beneath the surface, deep rearrangements are taking place.

Energies are recalibrating. Patterns are loosening. Old roots are dying back to make space for stronger ones. The soul, like the seed, is responding to signals far subtler than logic. These cycles are not failures. They are initiations.

To honor the seed within is to stop forcing yourself to bloom out of season. It is to recognize that your unfolding cannot be rushed or replicated. That your path may look different from others not because you are behind, but because you are honoring a different geometry of becoming. A geometry that remembers something older than your personality. Something wiser than your plans.

Even the obstacles that seem to block your way are part of the code. The stone that cracks the seed shell. The weight of the soil that teaches strength. The darkness that forces direction. Nothing in nature grows in a straight line. Every twist, every pause, every detour has meaning. Not as moral lesson, but as structure. The path is not arbitrary. It is encoded with memory.

And this memory is not limited to your own lifetime. Just as the tree remembers forests that no longer stand, you carry threads from beyond your individual story. Lineage. Myth. Collective memory. The ache you feel for a world you've never seen may not be imagination. It may be remembrance. The knowing of the seed reaching for the shape of its original tree. The blueprint of wholeness held quietly in the dark.

The longing you feel for meaning, for depth, for a life aligned with something unspoken, is not a deficiency. It is the signal of memory. A cellular awareness that you are meant for more than consumption, performance, and exhaustion. This longing does not seek comfort. It seeks coherence. Not comfort in the form of ease, but the deeper comfort of resonance. The rightness that emerges when your life begins to mirror the shape of your soul.

That shape is not constructed through effort. It is revealed through alignment. Just as the seed does not calculate how to grow roots, stems, leaves, fruit, or flower, you are not meant to engineer your essence. You are meant to remove what blocks its unfolding. Conditioning. Self-doubt. Hyper-identification with survival patterns. These are the weeds that choke the signal, the noise that confuses instinct.

The remembering process begins not with action, but with stillness. A listening that is neither passive nor impatient. It requires a willingness to stop trying to fix what was never broken and instead tune into the rhythm that pulses underneath the distortions. That rhythm often comes through silence. Through presence. Through a kind of radical honesty that cuts through the noise and brings you face-to-face with what has always been waiting to rise.

Many fear this level of presence because it requires a kind of death. Not a literal one, but the death of false identities. The death of the masks you've worn to survive. The death of the roles you've clung to for belonging. But this is not annihilation. It is germination. It is the cracking of the seed's shell. Painful, yes. But essential. You cannot grow into your truth without shedding what is no longer true.

There is a particular kind of courage needed here. Not the courage of bold declarations or public transformation, but the quiet, inward courage to stop pretending. To sit with the discomfort of not knowing. To allow grief its full expression. To acknowledge that some of what you've built may need to fall away, not because you failed, but because it was never meant to last. It served its time, and now something older is ready to emerge.

This emergence is not dramatic. It is often tender. Gentle. Almost imperceptible. Like the first green shoot pushing through the soil. It does not need validation. It does not seek applause. It simply knows its way upward, because it has always known. The code is intact. The intelligence is whole. You do not need to be taught your true path. You need to stop interrupting it.

To live this way is to move from essence, not identity. From presence, not performance. It is to realize that the same wisdom that governs the tides and the stars also pulses in your chest. You are not separate from the intelligence of the tree. You are an extension of it. The same laws apply. The same rhythm guides.

And like the tree, you are not here for speed. You are here for depth. For rootedness. For fruit that feeds something greater than you. The seed never hoards what it becomes. The tree offers itself freely. Shade, fruit, oxygen, shelter. Its fulfillment is not in how much it grows, but in how fully it gives what it was meant to give. This is true success. Not accumulation, but contribution. Not dominance, but harmony.

The remembering of the seed is not a return to the past. It is a return to the original frequency before distortion. A return to what was always whole, always clear, always enough. When you live from this place, your choices become aligned. Your energy flows without friction. Life no longer feels like something you must chase or conquer. It becomes something you co-create. A conversation between your essence and the living world.

The seed does not need to become the tree. It already is. It only needs to be placed in the right conditions. So it is with you. You are not waiting to become. You are remembering how to allow.

# The Light That Waits in the Ashes

*There is a silence that follows destruction. Not the silence of peace, but the stillness that comes when the fire has finished consuming. When what was once known has been reduced to soot and memory. In that silence, the mind often panics. It wants to rebuild immediately, to fix, to patch, to escape the unbearable void. But true transformation does not rush. The ashes are not the end. They are a beginning in disguise.*

---

Every human life carries its season of burning. These are not always visible from the outside. Sometimes they come as external losses. Other times, as internal unraveling. A crumbling of certainty. A collapse of who you thought you were. The identities you wore like armor fall to the ground. And beneath them, there is only dust.

This is the place most people fear. Not because it is empty, but because it is unfamiliar. It strips away the known. It offers no quick comfort, no clear answers. And yet, it is in this barren space that something sacred starts to stir. Not something you create. Something that has been waiting.

The light does not appear as a flash or a flare. It does not shout. It is quiet, patient, and unwavering. It sits beneath the charred remains, beneath the illusions that had to die. It is not born of avoidance. It is born of honesty. The kind of honesty that can only be accessed when all distractions are gone. In this place, you begin to see what truly matters. The masks fall away. The noise of the world loses its grip. And the deeper rhythm of life begins to emerge. A rhythm that is not driven by ambition or appearance, but by essence. The light in the ashes is not a reward for suffering. It is the return to what was always real. A purity unshaken by circumstance.

But to reach it, you must be willing to sit in the dark. You must resist the urge to rebuild too soon. Many rush to replace what burned without understanding what it meant. They recreate the same patterns in a new form, layering distraction over pain. But if you stay with the ashes, if you do not flinch from their truth, you may notice a different kind of emergence.

Not a return to who you were, but a revelation of who you are. Not a rebuilding of the past, but a recognition of something that was never built. The light is not new. It is ancient. It lives in the core of your being. But sometimes it takes fire to uncover it.

The fire reveals by removing. It removes the inessential, the artificial, the inherited scripts. It shows you what can no longer survive and, in doing so, makes space for what can finally live. This is the paradox of loss. It devastates and liberates. It wounds and awakens. It is not something to be sought, but when it comes, it can be entered with reverence.

Not all who burn are broken. Some are being reshaped. Not all who fall are lost. Some are being returned to ground so that something truer can rise. But this rising is not loud. It is not dramatic. It does not look like triumph. It looks like stillness. A quiet knowing. A sense of returning home without moving.

This is where the light begins to gather. In the soft recognition that what was lost was never the source. The source remains, untouched by the flame. Waiting for your eyes to clear, for your breath to slow, for your heart to open wide enough to receive it.

The return to this light is not a process of effort. It is a surrender. A melting of the last inner resistance that clings to what has already fallen. The identity that was built on survival, on pleasing, on protection, cannot walk with you into this space. It cannot carry the silence. It cannot bear the weight of what is real.

You do not need to know what comes next to allow this presence to rise. In fact, knowing is often the very thing that keeps it hidden. It rises when there is no strategy left. No image to maintain. No script to follow. It rises when your only prayer is truth, no matter how bare it feels.

The mind may try to make meaning from the ashes, to turn them into a story of strength or heroism. But this light does not need justification. It does not perform. It does not seek attention. It simply is. And its being is enough to reorient your entire sense of self. What was once driven by the need to be seen is now rooted in the knowing that you are already seen. Not by others, but by the field of existence itself.

In this space, time bends. What once felt urgent no longer matters. What once consumed you begins to dissolve. The past, with all its echoes, loosens its grip. And for the first time, you may feel what it is to be fully here. Unguarded. Not performing. Not surviving. Simply present.

This presence does not come through striving. It arrives through letting go. Letting go of the need to fix yourself. Letting go of the belief that healing must be dramatic. Letting go of the idea that awakening must be loud. It is none of these things. It is soft. It is slow. It is steady.

You become a vessel that no longer leaks. A space where silence can expand without being chased away. A body that no longer flinches from its own sensation. A mind that no longer trembles at the unknown. And in that quiet expansion, you feel something move through you that was never of your making.

This is not a metaphor. It is a lived reality. The light in the ashes is not symbolic. It is energetic. It is the return of coherence. The return of alignment. The return of a center that was buried under the rubble of the conditioned self. You do not need to invent it. You only need to uncover what was already encoded into your being.

There is no map for this. There is only attention. There is only the willingness to stay awake when you would rather numb. To breathe into the places that feel scorched. To touch the grief without needing it to disappear. To hold the confusion without demanding clarity. These are not small things. They are initiations.

The ones who walk through the ashes without pretending are the ones who emerge carrying a different kind of power. Not the power to dominate or convince. The power to see clearly. To feel without fear. To move without distortion. They become the living temple for what cannot be spoken, only felt.

You are not meant to rebuild what burned. You are meant to listen to what the fire revealed. To carry the ember forward, not the structure. To honor the loss without worshiping the past. This is how light moves in the world now. Quietly. Through those who have nothing left to prove.

The light that waits in the ashes is not outside you. It is you, stripped of all that was never yours. It is not what you gain. It is what remains when everything else falls away. And it is more whole than anything you could ever construct.

Let it rise. Not with noise, but with presence. Not with force, but with truth. Let it become the breath you did not know you were holding. Let it speak in silence, walk without effort, love without condition. Let it remind you, as only light can, that you were never lost. You were simply covered.

And now, without needing to be found, you begin to see.

# Chapter VIII: The Circle That Has No End

### The Law of Return in All Things

*There is a hidden symmetry at the heart of existence. It is not always visible to the eyes, nor is it easily grasped by the rational mind, yet it governs the movement of all things. This symmetry is the law of return. It is the quiet rhythm beneath creation, the pulse that brings all things back to their source. Not as they were, but as they have been transformed.*

---

The law of return does not mean repetition. It is not a cycle in which we endlessly replay the same story. Instead, it is an intelligence embedded in life itself, where each movement outward is matched by a movement inward. Every breath, every heartbeat, every season carries within it this arc of expansion and return. The inhale does not continue forever. The tide does not stay in its fullness. The seed does not remain in bloom. All things rise, and all things fold back into stillness.

What returns is not the same as what left. And this is the subtle power of the law. It is not about going back. It is about integration. The return brings with it the lessons, the imprints, the changed form of the journey. And in doing so, it offers us the chance to meet the origin again, not as who we were, but as who we have become.

This law plays out in your body. Your nervous system is shaped by patterns of return. The stress that leaves unprocessed will always seek a way back. The grief not fully felt will echo through other moments until it is honored. Emotions do not simply vanish. They move in spirals, calling you into contact with what remains unresolved. Not as punishment, but as invitation.

In relationships, too, this law is alive. The dynamics you run from often show up in new faces. The unmet part of you will call in mirrors until it is seen. The return is not there to shame you. It is there to guide you. It brings back what you abandoned, so that you may carry it differently. With more presence. With more wisdom. With more love.

The ancients understood this law not just as a pattern of nature, but as a sacred principle. They knew that every act carried a thread, and that thread would eventually be woven back into the one who began it. Not as judgment, but as completion. This is why prayer was not just an appeal, but a tuning. A re-alignment with the spiral. A way to walk in harmony with what would inevitably return.

You are not separate from this rhythm. Even in the moments when you feel furthest from yourself, furthest from truth, something within you is already turning back. There is an instinct deeper than the mind that knows how to return. It may not speak in words. It may not offer comfort. But it moves. And that movement, however quiet, is what brings you home.

To resist the return is to hold yourself in a space of perpetual contraction. It is to cling to the illusion that forward is the only direction that matters. But healing is not linear. Awakening is not a straight ascent. They both require descent. They require circling back through what has been disowned, misunderstood, forgotten.

This is why the same fears reappear, the same doubts re-surface, the same wounds pulse again at new thresholds. It is not because you are failing. It is because something essential is calling to be carried across the threshold with you. Not left behind, but honored. This is the medicine of return.

You cannot ascend without roots. And your roots are found in the soil of your lived experience. To deny that experience is to sever your own line of growth. But to return to it, to re-enter it with new awareness, is to reclaim the energy that has been held in waiting.

When you allow yourself to re-enter those buried places, you begin to dissolve the tension that holds your energy in loops of avoidance. What once appeared as blocks or failures begins to reveal itself as hidden intelligence, shaping the exact conditions needed for integration. The pain that seemed like a detour becomes the pathway. The memory you resisted becomes a key.

This is not a mental process. The law of return operates at the level of pattern and presence. The body often knows it before the mind is willing. You may find yourself drawn back to an old place, a forgotten practice, or a conversation long overdue. You may wake in the night with the echo of something left unspoken years ago. These are not signs of regression. They are signs of life responding to life, of the field inviting you to close the loop. There is an art to receiving the return. It asks for stillness, not passivity. It asks for courage, not analysis. It asks for the kind of inner silence that allows the return to complete its work. You cannot force this spiral. You can only enter into resonance with it.

Some people spend their entire lives running from the return. They reinvent themselves at every threshold, hoping to escape what waits beneath the surface. But what is unprocessed does not disappear. It waits. It gathers weight in the unconscious until it shapes reality itself. The longer it is postponed, the more distorted it becomes. Not to punish, but to intensify the call to return.

Others make the mistake of clinging to the past, mistaking nostalgia for sacred memory. But the law of return is not about longing for what was. It is about retrieving what was lost in a way that can serve who you are now. It is about memory becoming presence. About experience becoming embodiment.

To truly walk with this law is to stop seeing your path as a straight line toward an imagined future. It is to see your path as a spiral, drawing you deeper into the center of yourself, again and again. Each loop brings a higher view, but also a more intimate contact with what lies beneath. The deeper you go, the wider your capacity becomes to hold paradox, to move with the seasons of your being, to welcome what comes and what returns.

At the mystical level, the law of return is a cosmic pattern. Stars collapse back into themselves. Galaxies arc through space only to be drawn inward again. The entire universe is engaged in a great breath of becoming and returning. You are not separate from that. Your own cycles echo this larger intelligence.

In the soul's journey, this law appears as the return to essence. After all the masks, after all the seeking, after all the trials, the soul is called back to what it always was. Not to regress, but to remember. Not to dissolve, but to be distilled. Every experience, every sorrow, every joy becomes part of the refinement. Nothing is wasted. Nothing is outside the spiral.

There are moments when this return feels like death. A shedding of identity so complete that it leaves you disoriented. But these deaths are sacred. They are the gateways to a fuller form of life. In the alchemical traditions, this dissolution was the necessary stage before the gold could appear. The chaos, the uncertainty, the emptiness are not errors. They are thresholds.

To resist the return is to harden. To surrender to it is to allow the sacred rhythm to shape you. You do not lose yourself by returning. You regain the thread that was always yours. And with it, you move forward not as someone new, but as someone whole.

The law of return is not a punishment, not a trap, not a repetition. It is grace in motion. It is the hidden spiral that brings your life into coherence. And once you begin to walk with it consciously, you discover that nothing real is ever lost. It only waits to be brought back into light, through you.

## The Spiral Beyond the Line

*There is a subtle illusion that lingers in the modern mind: the idea that life is a line. A progression from beginning to end. A ladder to climb. A series of milestones to reach and then leave behind.*

---

This idea is deeply ingrained in the way most people interpret growth, success, time, even healing. It appears rational, orderly, comforting in its simplicity. Yet, beneath that simplicity lies a distortion that can quietly fracture one's relationship with the deeper truth of becoming.

The soul does not grow by linear advancement. It unfolds in spirals.

This distinction is not a poetic metaphor. It is a precise description of how transformation actually moves through your life. When you begin to see this, the events you once considered setbacks or regressions take on a different meaning. They reveal themselves not as detours but as returns. Not as failures, but as part of a greater rhythm.

The spiral honors depth. It does not seek to escape the past, but to revisit it from a higher vantage. Each turn of the spiral takes you back to familiar ground, but never in the same way. You encounter the same pattern, the same fear, the same longing, but you are different now. What could not be seen or held before becomes available. What once collapsed you now reveals a doorway. The spiral brings you not back, but through.

Linear thinking resists this. It judges the reappearance of old wounds as a flaw in your process. It measures your worth by distance covered. And so it drives you to perform healing rather than inhabit it, to collect achievements instead of deepen presence. The spiral dissolves this pressure. It returns you to the same inner threshold again and again, not to torment you, but to liberate what still remains entangled.

This is why some of your most powerful shifts happen quietly, invisibly. Not through dramatic change, but through subtle reorientation. A moment in which you respond to the familiar with unfamiliar softness. A day when you speak the truth you used to avoid. An evening where you no longer betray yourself in the same way. On the surface, these moments might seem small. In the spiral, they are everything.

There is intelligence in the spiral that cannot be grasped by the intellect. It follows a rhythm deeper than logic. It is the pattern of galaxies, of shells, of hurricanes, of sacred architecture. It is encoded in your DNA. It shapes the seasons of nature and the seasons of the psyche. You are not separate from it. You are woven into it.

To walk the spiral consciously is to allow mystery back into the process. It is to stop seeking only progress and begin listening for depth. It is to recognize that presence does not accumulate like currency, but returns to itself in ever-refined expressions. The more you attune to this, the less you need to prove that you are moving forward. You begin to feel when you are moving inward. That is the true direction of the spiral: not up or down, but toward the center.

The mind, conditioned by years of striving, will try to reduce this to a goal. But the spiral is not a goal. It is a mode of being. It invites you to see yourself not as a project to complete, but as a temple being built from the inside out. Each loop of the spiral clears a deeper layer, carves a deeper passage, unveils a deeper memory of what you are. And just as you glimpse the center, the spiral opens again.

This is the paradox of true movement. You may find yourself in the same place, facing the same conditions, with the same memories stirring, but if you listen closely, you'll notice the resonance has changed. You are not standing where you once stood, even if all appearances suggest so. Something within you has widened, softened, deepened. What once felt like confinement now feels like an invitation. The spiral has turned again.

In this way, evolution is rarely explosive. It is not a loud, final departure from what came before. It is a subtle refinement of perception. You are not breaking free from the past but reweaving your relationship to it. You begin to see how even the most painful threads were carrying the same longing for truth, for home, for reunion with the sacred center. There is no need to discard your former selves. They are not in the way. They are the way.

The spiral teaches reverence for process. Not because it demands patience, but because it reveals how every part of your path, even the crooked or collapsed ones, held codes for your return. Nothing was wasted. Even delay carries instruction. Even stillness is movement in disguise. When you begin to trust this, you no longer panic at the reappearance of doubt or disorientation. You meet it with the quiet knowing that you have met it before and you are meeting it differently now.

This is not regression. It is recursion. A sacred repetition with variation. Life is not testing you. Life is dialoguing with you. It shows you the same symbol again because it is unfolding in greater nuance. It brings the same lesson not because you failed, but because you are now ready to embody it more fully. In the spiral, recurrence is a sign of readiness, not failure. It is a whisper that says, "You can hold more now."

Linear time resists this truth. It places value on leaving things behind. But wisdom is not measured by what you've left. It is revealed by how deeply you can return to what remains and meet it with new presence. The spiral offers you this doorway again and again until there is no part of you left outside the temple. Until you can walk through the ruins of your former self with nothing but gentleness.

To integrate this way of seeing requires humility. The willingness to let go of the illusion of final arrival. The willingness to meet your own becoming as something holy and unfinished. The spiral does not end. It dissolves the notion of ends entirely. It invites you to stop chasing the horizon and begin listening to the ground beneath your feet. This moment, this breath, this return, is not less than progress. It is the place where the sacred meets you. And when the spiral touches the deepest part of you, you may notice that what you once called transformation is really remembrance. The change was not into something new but into something truer. The path was not a climb but a circling back to what never left. The spiral does not add to you. It reveals you. It does not make you greater. It makes you whole.

This is why true wisdom often sounds like simplicity. Not because it is easy, but because it has passed through the spiral of complexity and returned home. It no longer needs to impress or prove. It simply is. And in that being, it becomes the mirror in which others remember themselves too.

You are not here to escape your patterns. You are here to move through them in a new rhythm. You are not here to erase your history. You are here to inhabit it differently. The spiral is the path that honors every step and every return. Not as detours, not as delays, but as the very architecture of awakening. You do not walk it to become worthy. You walk it because you already are.

And every time you spiral inward, the center breathes more fully through you. Until there is no more path to follow. Only presence to embody.

## Time as a Mirror, Not a Chain

*Time has long been perceived as a linear force, an arrow pointing forward, dragging us from birth to death in a straight and unyielding line. It is taught to us as something external, mechanical, something that happens to us. The clock ticks, the calendar turns, and we are expected to keep up. Within this frame, time becomes a chain — an invisible restraint around the soul. It marks how late we are, how much we've missed, how far we are from where we think we should be.*
*But time, in its true nature, is not a tyrant. It is a mirror.*

---

It does not pull us forward like a leash, nor does it trap us in its structure. It reflects. Not the hours or the years, but the essence of our own becoming. Time mirrors our consciousness. It bends, expands, slows, or accelerates in response to our presence. You may notice that in moments of deep clarity or joy, time seems to dissolve. Minutes stretch into eternity. Conversely, when your mind is fragmented or rushed, hours vanish in a blur. Time obeys perception. It does not govern it.

The idea that time is objective is one of the great illusions of modern thought. This illusion serves a world built on schedules, deadlines, and production. But it does not serve the soul. The soul moves cyclically. It listens to seasons, not seconds. Its wisdom unfolds in spirals, not straight lines. And when we begin to align with that inner rhythm, we start to see that what we call "past" and "future" are simply mirrors positioned at different angles, each reflecting a part of us waiting to be met.

This is why unresolved pain from ten years ago can still feel raw. It has not traveled anywhere. It is not "behind" you in some distant archive of time. It is here, alive, because your consciousness has circled back to it. And likewise, dreams that seem far off in the "future" may already be brushing up against you, waiting for your eyes to open. Time does not separate you from what matters. It reveals how close you are.

When you begin to see time in this way, healing takes on a different shape. You no longer try to outrun your past or rush toward a better version of yourself. Instead, you turn to meet the reflection time offers. You let it show you what has been buried, what has been postponed, what you are ready to integrate now. Each moment becomes an invitation, not an obligation.

This shift requires inner stillness. Not the absence of movement, but the kind of stillness that lets you see clearly. When you're no longer racing the clock, you can begin to observe what time is showing you. You'll start to notice how certain patterns recur, not as punishment, but as sacred signals. Time is not looping against you. It is holding up the mirror again and again until you see yourself clearly, without distortion.

The fear of wasted time begins to fade. You realize that nothing was truly wasted, because every detour brought you closer to this recognition. Even years spent in confusion or avoidance become part of the pattern. They are folded into the spiral of your return. Time is not measuring your success. It is offering you a reflection of where your consciousness currently stands in relation to truth.

At this point, many begin to ask: if time is a mirror, then how do we interact with it intentionally, rather than reactively? That is where the deeper path begins.

You begin by watching, not rushing. Watch how certain emotions flare at particular times of the day. Observe how your energy rises or dips in rhythm with the moon, the sun, the seasons. These are not arbitrary shifts. They are feedback loops between you and the deeper layers of time, the ones that do not tick but pulse. When you listen this way, you realize that time speaks. It has always been trying to get your attention, not to trap you in routine, but to awaken your sensitivity to presence.

Presence collapses the illusion of distance. What you feared would take years to unfold may unfold in a single instant of deep awareness. Insight does not require the passage of time. It requires the permission to see what was already waiting. In that moment, what was once past pain becomes present truth. What seemed like a distant vision becomes lived reality. Time bends, not as a trick of perception, but as a reflection of where your consciousness has landed.

This is why awakening can feel both sudden and ancient. You remember something you never intellectually knew, and yet it feels more familiar than your name. That memory is not bound to a year or a life. It lives in the architecture of your soul, and time is the mirror that brings it back into view. You do not become something new. You become aware of what has always been held inside you. And once seen, it cannot be unseen.

There is no need to fight with clocks. You are not running out of time. That is a distortion whispered by fear. What you are running out of is fragmentation. The scattered sense of being pulled in all directions, with no center. The more whole you become, the less concerned you are with racing toward milestones. Your life becomes a rhythm, not a race.

And in this rhythm, synchronicity becomes natural. You find yourself in the right place at the right moment, not because you planned perfectly, but because your inner timing has aligned with the deeper field. What you seek starts to seek you, not out of magic but out of resonance. The mirror of time reflects coherence. And when you are coherent, your path unfolds with fewer detours, not because the world has changed, but because your perception no longer distorts the signal.

This way of being demands trust. Not the passive kind that waits for the universe to hand you comfort, but the active trust that allows discomfort to serve its purpose. When time delays something, it is not always a denial. Sometimes it is a refining. A clearing. A preparation. Time stretches not to punish but to shape. If you allow it, you will see how every pause contains an intelligence deeper than your plans.

The spiral of time does not move in repetition, but in expansion. You return to familiar lessons, not to suffer them again, but to see them from higher ground. What felt like failure years ago now reveals its gift. What you resisted comes back as an ally. The mirror does not lie, but it does wait. And when you are ready to see what it has always shown, you will find that time has not been lost. It has been storing the fragments of your self, waiting for you to gather them.

You are not late. You are not behind. You are in rhythm with a pattern so vast, so intricate, that only presence can reveal it. The wisdom of time is not in how much you can do within it, but in how deeply you can meet it. When you stop measuring life in hours and start meeting it in essence, you stop aging in fear and begin unfolding in truth.

Time has never been your master. It has only ever been your mirror. And now that you can see your reflection with clarity, you are free to walk without chains, in a rhythm that belongs only to you.

# Chapter IX: The Tongue That Speaks Without Sound

## The Language of Symbols

*The universe does not speak in paragraphs. It speaks in patterns, images, echoes, and silence. It speaks in symbols. While words fragment reality into sequences, symbols collapse complexity into essence. They are the architecture beneath language, older than writing, older than speech. A symbol is not merely a sign; it is a container. It does not explain — it transmits.*

---

This is why sacred traditions have always relied on symbols, not to hide knowledge, but to preserve it. What is hidden is not obscured out of cruelty. It is protected from dilution. A symbol preserves a multidimensional truth in a form that transcends time, culture, and linear logic. The initiate is not taught what a symbol means. They are taught how to approach it.

Meaning arises not from decoding, but from resonance. A symbol reveals only what the observer is ready to see. That is why symbols feel alive. They meet you where you are and then invite you deeper. The more you evolve, the more a single symbol can open. A circle may first seem like a shape. Later it becomes a womb, a cycle, a return, an unbroken presence. Nothing in the symbol changes. But you do. And that is the hidden dialogue it has been waiting for.

When you learn to read symbols, you are not learning a new language. You are remembering an old one. A child instinctively draws the sun with lines radiating outward. They draw eyes as windows. They create stories with shapes before they ever write sentences. Symbolic thought is innate. It is the raw language of the soul before it is trained into linear cognition.

Modern minds, obsessed with precision, often fear symbols. They demand one-to-one correspondence, fixed definitions, empirical clarity. But the nature of a symbol is precisely what escapes the net of rational control. It is not vague — it is layered. It is not confusing — it is expansive. The intellect may feel uncomfortable in its presence, but the heart recognizes its familiarity.

This is why dreams, visions, and archetypes often come in symbolic form. Consciousness does not rely solely on waking thoughts to process the unseen. It speaks in a different cadence at night, when the rational gatekeeper softens. A staircase in a dream is not just architecture. It may be an invitation to ascend inwardly. A flood may not be weather. It may be emotion that the conscious mind refuses to feel.

To dismiss these symbols as "just dreams" is to turn your back on the deepest mirror you possess. The symbolic realm is where the soul does its work, speaking in images because words are too slow, too narrow. And yet, this symbolic intelligence is not separate from waking life. It spills into art, into intuition, into moments of déjà vu, into the shapes and rhythms that pull you in without explanation.

Once you begin to pay attention, the entire world shifts. A bird landing beside you at a crossroads is no longer random. A number repeating itself in different places becomes a thread. A pattern of events carries a rhythm you can feel but cannot explain. You do not become superstitious. You become attuned. The difference is presence. Superstition reacts in fear. Attunement responds in awareness.

Your capacity to understand symbols is directly linked to your capacity to hold mystery without rushing to collapse it. Mystery is not confusion. It is unspoken fullness. And symbols protect that fullness, not by obscuring it, but by requiring reverence from the one who would enter. The way you approach a symbol shapes what it will reveal. If you demand it to behave like a fact, it may remain silent. If you approach it like a living teacher, it begins to open.

This is the threshold of symbolic wisdom: where meaning is not extracted, but received. Where you do not own the truth, but are shaped by it. Where the mind begins to kneel and the heart begins to hear.

There is a moment when the symbol ceases to be external and begins to mirror the interior. This is the crossing point where knowledge becomes knowing. A symbol, once contemplated, does not just remain an object of study. It imprints itself within the psyche, drawing forth reflections that language cannot hold. The interaction becomes alchemical. It does not merely inform — it transforms.

This is why sacred symbols are not explained in esoteric traditions, but meditated upon. The purpose is not to define the symbol but to dissolve the boundaries between the observer and the observed. When this happens, the symbol stops being an icon and starts being an initiation. You are no longer separate from the pattern. You realize you have always carried it.

A serpent consuming its tail is not simply an ancient motif. It is the presence of a cycle that contains its own rebirth. It speaks of completion, return, self-sustenance, and eternal motion. The symbol is not meant to be dissected. It is meant to be absorbed. In that absorption, you are reminded of a deeper rhythm inside your life. The mind may not grasp it entirely, but something in you aligns with it.

This is the true function of the symbolic: to realign the fragmented self with the totality. When your life feels disjointed, meaningless, or mechanical, it is not answers you lack, but symbols. Without them, you interpret life only through logic or memory. With them, you begin to navigate by resonance and presence. A symbol is a compass of the invisible. It guides not by dictating direction but by amplifying recognition.

You begin to notice how every tradition carries its own sacred lexicon — a constellation of forms that preserve its wisdom. The lotus. The spiral. The staff. The wheel. These are not decorations. They are embodiments of truths so expansive that they had to be distilled into shapes. The sacred geometry that underlies them is not a coincidence of aesthetics. It is a reflection of universal law.

When you feel drawn to a certain symbol, do not rush to interpret it. Let it work on you. Observe what memories it stirs, what emotions it evokes, what dreams begin to shift around it. You may find that it calls forth a part of you you had forgotten, or never fully known. This is not psychological projection. It is the resonance of an ancient recognition that precedes biography.

At this level, you no longer try to manipulate symbols. You surrender to them. They become doorways, not trophies. They do not exist for decoration, nor to be worn as empty fashion. They require a posture of humility, of stillness, of listening. If they are to offer revelation, they demand presence. And this presence is the beginning of spiritual literacy.

Eventually, you discover that your life itself begins to function symbolically. Events do not just happen. They arrange themselves with precision.

Encounters carry echoes. Timing becomes uncanny. What seemed random begins to feel orchestrated. Not in a deterministic way, but in a way that reveals underlying harmony. You are no longer separate from the intelligence that weaves the symbols. You are woven into them.

To live in this way is not to abandon logic or reason, but to restore their place within a larger field of knowing. The intellect becomes a servant, not a master. And the symbolic becomes a bridge — between the visible and the invisible, the known and the ineffable. It is here that truth is not asserted, but unveiled. It is not explained, but embodied.

The language of symbols does not ask you to believe. It invites you to remember. Not as memory of facts, but as a return to the pulse of meaning that has always moved beneath the surface of things. This pulse has a shape. It speaks. And it is listening.

## Dreams as Sacred Transmissions

*Most people treat dreams as mere fragments of the mind, strange narratives born of stress, memory, or emotion. But in the deeper traditions, dreams are not seen as byproducts of the psyche — they are recognized as transmissions. Sacred, purposeful, and coded with meaning. They arrive not from the surface mind, but from a deeper stratum of consciousness that speaks in symbol and rhythm. To receive a dream is not to hallucinate while sleeping. It is to be spoken to by the unseen.*

---

In many ancient cultures, dreams were the language of the divine. The Egyptians understood them as doorways between worlds. The Greeks built temples of incubation, where people would sleep to receive healing visions from gods. Shamans across continents used dreams not only for guidance but to travel, to locate illness, to receive instruction from the spirits of plants, animals, or ancestors. In these lineages, the dreamer was never passive. She was an initiate.

The modern world, having reduced consciousness to neurological function, has largely stripped dreams of their sacred weight. They are analyzed, diagnosed, or dismissed. But this dismissal is a symptom of forgetting. When dreams are seen as static content to be interpreted or filed away, we lose access to their living essence. We forget that they are alive while we are sleeping. That they do not simply entertain the mind, but touch the soul.

A true dream is not linear. It bends time, warps logic, and challenges identity because it is not constrained by waking rules. It speaks the language of archetypes, of symbols, of felt but often unspoken truths. A snake in a dream may not be a literal danger or a personal fear. It may be a carrier of energy, an agent of transformation, a coded whisper from the unconscious. These images do not explain — they initiate.

To understand dreams, you must approach them not as puzzles to be solved, but as messengers to be honored. This requires a different posture. Not analysis, but receptivity. Not judgment, but listening. A sacred dream does not yield its meaning to the intellect. It reveals itself over time, through resonance, synchronicity, and recognition. The meaning is not extracted — it is lived into.

When you begin to treat your dreams as transmissions, your relationship with sleep itself changes. It is no longer a place of escape or recovery. It becomes a temple. And you enter it with intention. This is not about technique, but orientation. You go to bed not just to rest the body, but to open the gate between dimensions. To invite the deep voice of your being to speak in a form that cannot be censored by the waking mind.

Some dreams arrive as visions. Others as riddles. Some echo with clarity, others dissolve upon waking. All are offerings. Not every dream is cosmic or life-changing, but each has a signature, a frequency, a texture. When you begin to attune yourself, even the simplest dream can deliver a profound shift. The key is not to rush into interpretation. It is to hold the dream as you would a sacred text — patiently, reverently, openly.

There are dreams that come once and never return, but leave a mark forever. Others repeat with slight variation, trying to be heard. Some appear meaningless until a day, a month, or a year later, when life brings a moment that mirrors them perfectly. This is when you realize: the dream knew before you did.

There is a certain humility required to receive dreams without demanding immediate understanding. The soul does not speak in straight lines. It speaks in waves, in impressions, in metaphors that unfold through the body as much as the mind. A dream may bypass your logic entirely and instead press itself into your bones. It may leave behind a mood, a sensation, a knowing that cannot be named but refuses to leave. These are not byproducts to be brushed off. They are traces of transmission.

To walk the path of the awakened dreamer is not to become a perfect interpreter. It is to become a vessel. This means tending to the relationship. It means creating space in your waking life to receive what your sleeping life is offering. Silence helps. So does writing, not to dissect, but to preserve. A dream journal is not a workbook. It is a reliquary. Each recorded dream, even if fragmentary, builds a bridge between worlds. The more you honor the language of the dreamtime, the more fluently it begins to speak.

Over time, a sacred rhythm emerges. You begin to recognize when a dream carries the scent of prophecy. When it comes with a tone of warning. When it reflects your inner architecture or cracks open an old emotional seal. Some dreams arrive like initiations, pulling you into an underworld descent or a radiant ascent. Others come as clear mirrors, showing you what the waking ego refuses to acknowledge. And some do not speak to your personal story at all. They are collective, ancestral, cosmic. These dreams are not yours alone. You are simply the receiver.

There is a kind of spiritual maturity that forms when you stop needing your dreams to make sense. When you let them move through you, even when they confuse or unsettle. Many initiates have learned more from a dream that broke them open than from a thousand hours of study. The dream speaks in the dialect of the soul precisely because it cannot be controlled. That is its power. It slips past the gatekeeper of rationality and touches what you did not know was waiting to be remembered.

This is why dreams have been feared and suppressed by regimes of control. A dream can make you question the rules of time. It can carry messages that contradict what society claims is true. It can give you knowledge no one else sees. Not because you are special, but because you are listening. This capacity to receive is dangerous to systems that depend on passive, unquestioning minds. But to the awakened being, it is sacred responsibility. The most important dreams often feel the strangest. They disturb the tidy narrative. They scramble identity. They come cloaked in images that resist easy translation. This is not a flaw. This is how transmission works when it reaches beyond the edge of what your current self can contain. Your work is not to collapse it into meaning too soon, but to let it stretch you. Let it work on you like a slow fire. Let it show you who you were before you forgot.

Eventually, you will begin to dream not only for yourself, but for the whole. You will sense when a dream is part of a larger pattern. You will wake up with symbols that do not belong to your personal history, but to the spirit of the time. This is the territory of the oracle. Not as a role to claim, but as a function of being attuned. The dreamer becomes a witness. A channel. A translator of the deep.

In a world that is increasingly severed from mystery, to remember that dreaming is sacred is itself a revolutionary act. Not just because it connects you to ancient wisdom, but because it restores a relationship with the unseen. It reminds you that you are never alone in your unfolding. That even in the darkness, even in silence, the soul is always speaking.

And sometimes, the most important truths are whispered to you in sleep. Not to be explained. But to be carried. Carefully. Like a flame in the palm of your hand.

# Hearing with the Inner Flame

*There is a voice that does not speak in words. It does not rise from the tongue or vibrate through the air. It is not loud. It does not argue, explain, or demand. And yet, when it speaks, it cuts through noise with a clarity that no volume can match. This is the voice of the inner flame. Not the voice of thought or memory, not even the voice of intuition as commonly understood. It is deeper, quieter, and older. It belongs to the essence that watches your life from within.*

---

To hear this voice, one must first recognize that most of what we call "listening" is actually anticipation. We listen with expectation, waiting for confirmation of what we already believe. We listen through layers of identity, fear, and preference. But the inner flame cannot be heard through filters. It does not echo the ego. It does not speak to soothe your narrative. It speaks in presence. To hear it, you must become empty.

This kind of emptiness is not passive. It is alive. It is a clearing, not a void. It is not about muting your thoughts, but about loosening your grip on them. It is not about silencing the world, but about shifting the place from which you receive. The inner flame is always lit. The only question is whether you have become still enough to perceive its warmth, its flicker, its wisdom.

The ancient traditions knew this flame well. In the temples of Egypt, in the silence of Zen monasteries, in the desert wanderings of prophets and mystics, the inner fire was guarded not as metaphor, but as reality. It was seen as the indwelling presence of the divine, the axis around which perception itself could rotate. Those who cultivated this awareness were not just more insightful. They were more attuned to the living intelligence of reality itself.

In our modern world, that flame is rarely tended. We are taught to seek knowledge externally, to look for answers in data, formulas, consensus. And yet the deepest guidance cannot be taught. It must be remembered. It must be reclaimed from within. Not because it is hidden, but because it is subtle. And in a culture addicted to speed and spectacle, the subtle becomes invisible.

Hearing with the inner flame is not about receiving abstract messages or decoding riddles. It is about attunement. It is about being able to sense the difference between a path that depletes and a path that nourishes. Between a truth that liberates and a lie that comforts. It is the capacity to feel alignment before it becomes tangible. To recognize the yes or no of your being, not in thought, but in tone.

This tone is unmistakable once you know it. It may arrive as stillness in the chest, or a quiet drop in the belly, or a sudden clearing of mental fog. It might feel like a contraction, a lift, a breath that breathes you. It does not argue. It simply *is*. And it is always available, though rarely loud. It waits, not with urgency, but with patience. It knows that you will come when you are ready to listen without controlling.

When you begin to live from this place, everything changes. You start to make choices that are not based on fear, but on fire. You start to speak from a center that does not require validation. You no longer chase answers, because you begin to realize that the real task is not to collect knowledge, but to deepen listening.

This depth of listening is not passive observation. It is communion. The inner flame does not merely guide; it reveals. It exposes what is hollow, what is borrowed, what is no longer yours to carry. And in the same breath, it kindles remembrance. It lights up the hidden places where truth has long waited for your return. There is a kind of recognition that takes place when you listen this way. Not recognition of something new, but of something ancient that has always lived beneath the noise.

To hear with the inner flame is to step beyond the intellect and into a more primal intelligence. It is to lean into the current of life and feel where it flows clean and strong. Often, this will not match your plans. It may not fit your timing or your preferences. The flame does not speak to keep you comfortable. It speaks to keep you aligned. And sometimes, alignment requires surrendering the very structures you thought were essential.

This is why so many ignore the voice. Not because they cannot hear it, but because they fear where it might lead. The inner flame does not flatter. It does not bargain. It does not offer guarantees. It invites you into a path of authenticity that will burn away what is false. It is the flame, after all. To walk with it is to be purified, not in some ceremonial sense, but in the raw honesty of presence. There is no room for pretense where the flame burns clear.

But with this honesty comes a new kind of peace. A peace not based on outcomes, but on coherence. You begin to recognize the feeling of being in right relationship with yourself. Your steps may not always make sense to others. Your choices may defy logic or convenience. Yet they ring true, and that resonance becomes your compass. You are no longer performing life. You are inhabiting it. Fully, consciously, vulnerably.

There may be moments when the flame dims. When confusion sets in and silence stretches longer than you expected. This is not abandonment. It is often the space where deeper layers of self are being dissolved. When the flame seems far, it is usually burning in places you have not yet dared to enter. Do not chase it outward. Turn inward. Sit in the stillness. What feels like absence is often the preparation for deeper clarity.

And when the flame returns to the surface, when it speaks again, it will feel like a homecoming. Not because something external has resolved, but because you have rejoined yourself. You have remembered how to trust what cannot be measured. You have remembered that silence is not emptiness, but invitation. That guidance is not about control, but about attunement to the living current that flows through all things.

Over time, this way of hearing becomes less an act and more a state. You begin to carry the flame with you. It lives in your breath, your choices, your gaze. People around you may not know what has shifted, but they will feel it. There is a different kind of presence in one who listens from the center. A steadiness. A clarity that does not need to be proven. It speaks without needing to speak.

This is the quiet power of hearing with the inner flame. It is not about finding answers, but about learning how to dwell in the questions without collapsing. It is not about knowing more, but about needing less. It is not a path of acquisition, but of refinement. You become less distracted, more exact. Less performative, more real. And in that reality, the sacred becomes visible. Not as an idea, but as a lived frequency.

To hear with the inner flame is to remember who is truly listening. Not the self constructed from history and habit, but the essence that preceded all stories. The one who knows not through thought, but through direct contact with the eternal. And in this remembrance, the noise of the world softens. The fear of the unknown loosens its grip. You realize you were never alone in the silence. You were being called back to yourself, by the light that never left.

# Chapter X: The Breath Between Two Worlds

## Threshold States and Sacred Gaps

*There are moments in life that do not belong to the world of action or the world of rest. They are neither fully one thing nor the other. These are the threshold states, the in-between spaces where identity softens and the old rules seem to dissolve. They are not always dramatic or visible. Often, they appear quietly—after a loss, before a decision, in the hush between letting go and receiving. And yet, it is precisely in these ambiguous intervals that something essential begins to stir.*

---

Thresholds are uncomfortable because they strip away our illusions of certainty. In these liminal spaces, the familiar patterns no longer function, and the new ones have not yet formed. You can no longer pretend to be who you were, but you do not yet know who you are becoming. This is not failure. It is the fertile soil of true transformation. In the absence of structure, something ancient begins to breathe again. Not the voice of the self you've built, but the deeper current of what you've always been.

Modern life does not honor these spaces. It teaches us to fear the undefined, to rush through ambiguity, to fill the gaps with noise, productivity, or distraction. Yet spiritual tradition after spiritual tradition has pointed toward the same paradox: that it is in the space between things that the sacred becomes visible. The gap is not empty. It is full of presence, but not the kind you can control. It is the presence of what watches, what waits, what holds without demanding.

These in-between states are holy precisely because they invite surrender. You cannot force your way through a threshold. You cannot command clarity before its time. All you can do is remain present, aware, and open. This is what makes the gap sacred: it demands your full attention. Not to do anything, but to be with what is. To witness without grasping. To stay awake when everything inside wants to close down or speed up.

There is a silence that lives at the threshold. Not the silence of absence, but of depth. A silence that listens to you, that reflects back your unguarded self. If you allow yourself to dwell there, without trying to shape the next moment, you begin to sense a different kind of rhythm. Life is no longer linear. Time feels suspended. And in that suspension, something rearranges within you. You do not see it happening, but you will emerge changed.

What the threshold offers is not a plan, but a realignment. It strips away the roles, identities, and stories that once made sense but no longer fit. It does not replace them with new ones right away. First, it clears the space. This is the part most people resist. They want the clarity without the undoing. But true clarity cannot rise on top of distortion. It can only emerge from stillness, and stillness only comes when you stop reaching and start listening. Threshold states also hold memory—not memory as recollection, but as resonance. In these moments, you may feel flashes of something timeless: a scent, a sound, a knowing that is older than your personality. The gap becomes a place of remembering. Not just who you are becoming, but who you were before you forgot. This is not regression. It is integration. You are not going back. You are moving forward with your roots intact.

At some point, the silence shifts. A movement arises from within, not as instruction but as impulse. You feel drawn, nudged, not by pressure but by alignment. The gap begins to dissolve, not because you pushed through it, but because it has done its work. You have listened. You have waited. You have stayed with yourself long enough to see what is real. And now, something new begins to shape itself in you.

This kind of emergence carries a different texture than decision-making or strategy. It is not reactive, and it is not impulsive. It is born from contact with something vast, something beneath the ordinary mind. This is the wisdom of the sacred gap: it teaches you how to move from essence rather than habit. Your actions become quieter but more precise. Your direction feels less planned and more inevitable.

Those who learn to dwell in these liminal states begin to carry a certain depth. Not because they have more answers, but because they are less afraid of the unknown. They are not hurried by the discomfort of not knowing. They no longer see pauses as problems. They know that stillness is not stagnation, that silence is not absence, that waiting is not wasting. They become people who do not rush the sacred.

Many initiatory traditions preserved rites of passage specifically designed to place the initiate in these threshold states. The desert fast, the vision quest, the retreat into darkness—all were portals into the in-between. These rites were never just about endurance. They were about learning how to stand where nothing is fixed. To encounter the parts of oneself that only appear when everything else has been stripped away. And in that raw space, to meet something other.

What emerges from these experiences is not always immediately understandable. There is no guarantee of epiphany, no promise that the unknown will reveal itself in ways the rational mind can capture. Often what returns from the threshold is not a thought, but a shift in perception. A new way of seeing, subtle but irreversible. You find that your relationship to time has changed, or your idea of self feels softer, less bound. You realize that not everything must be solved. Some things must simply be lived.

The most potent thresholds are not always dramatic. They are often ordinary, hidden in plain sight. Waking up before dawn and sitting in the blue quiet. Standing at the edge of a major life change. Sitting with someone who is dying. Recovering from illness or heartbreak. Even moments of creative stagnation hold this power. These are the sacred gaps modern culture does not know how to honor, because they do not produce visible results. But results are not the point. Revelation is.

If you treat these moments as sacred, something begins to open. Not in the outer world, but in your attention. You become attuned to the spaces between words, the silence after a sentence, the breath between gestures. Life becomes less about the things and more about the spaces that hold them. These spaces teach you how to feel again. How to perceive from the inside out. How to recognize the echo of truth not in what is said, but in what is not said.

The sacred gap invites a different kind of listening, one that is not searching for information but allowing for communion. It requires no performance, no polishing, no proving. Just presence. When you meet life this way, the veils begin to thin. The world starts to speak differently. Patterns appear in places you never noticed. The wind has meaning. The delay becomes a message. The pause is no longer an absence, but a signal.

Eventually, the threshold releases you. Not because you found an answer, but because you became the one who could carry it. The person who entered the gap is not the one who leaves it. Something in you has died. Something else has rooted. The world feels new, not because it changed, but because you did. The sacred is no longer something you seek, but something you can now recognize. It lives in the cracks, the pauses, the spaces you once feared. And it speaks in a voice you now know how to hear.

# The Pause That Reveals

*There is a subtle intelligence that moves beneath the surface of life, one that cannot be accessed through speed or control. It reveals itself only in moments when the noise quiets, when the habitual rhythm breaks, when breath is held in stillness. In that space before the next motion, in the silence between gestures, something ancient watches and waits. The pause is not empty. It is not the absence of life. It is where life gathers itself.*

---

Modern culture despises the pause. It rushes to fill every gap with noise, movement, opinion, or distraction. The moment something slows, a reflex kicks in to fill it. We check our phones, scroll, talk, explain. We avoid the still point as if it might swallow us. But in the sacred traditions, that still point is the doorway. It is where the veil thins. It is where the hidden voice begins to speak.

To pause is not simply to stop. It is to become fully present in a space without forward momentum. Not withdrawing from life, but standing at the threshold of perception with all senses open. In such a state, awareness is not dulled by repetition. It becomes sharp, precise. You begin to see what is normally missed: the tension in a breath, the tremor behind a smile, the quiet meaning beneath the words. In the pause, things reveal themselves not because you analyze them, but because you are not rushing past them.

There are different kinds of pauses. Some arrive through grace, as in the stillness after witnessing something beautiful or devastating. Some are chosen, as in meditation or contemplation. Others are imposed by life itself: a sudden illness, a heartbreak, a loss, a delay. What unites them is the break in continuity. The familiar sequence halts, and something deeper is given the chance to emerge. Not every pause is pleasant. But every true pause contains the potential for revelation.

In esoteric traditions, the pause is often connected to the breath. The stillness at the top of the inhale. The suspension at the bottom of the exhale. These are not just biological moments. They are symbols of cosmic rhythms. The universe, too, breathes. Creation expands and contracts. Stars are born, collapse, and are born again. Even time itself has a pulse. The ancients knew that alignment with this rhythm was not achieved through force, but through attunement. Through learning how to dwell in the sacred intervals.

Many initiates speak of receiving insight not during rituals, but in the moments after them. Not during the peak of the practice, but in the silence that follows. It is as if the soul waits for a quiet hallway to deliver its message. The more profound the truth, the more softly it speaks. If you are still chasing noise, it will pass you by unnoticed. But if you have trained your attention to listen beyond the sound, it will reveal itself in full.

This is why many spiritual lineages regard silence not as the absence of speaking, but as a mode of listening. A discipline. A form of reverence. In the sacred pause, you are not merely waiting. You are becoming a vessel. You are making room for something greater to speak through you, something that does not use words. The pause does not interrupt life. It lets you finally hear what life has been saying all along.

You start to see that some answers do not come because you kept asking, but because you stopped asking. They needed space. They needed you to stop performing understanding and start receiving it. The pause becomes the container in which the unseen can take shape. The mystery does not fear being seen. It simply cannot be touched by hurried eyes. It reveals itself only when approached with stillness.

What begins to move is not a thought, not an emotion, not a conclusion. It is presence. A current of knowing without narration. It does not arrive to prove anything. It simply is. And from within that presence, clarity begins to arise, not as something you construct, but as something that always was. Like mist evaporating under sunlight, confusion fades, not because it was solved, but because the stillness allowed the deeper pattern to become visible.

This is the forgotten language of the pause. It does not speak to your intellect. It awakens the inner ear. The part of you that once knew how to sit beside the fire and feel the wisdom of night. The part that understood how to listen for the wind, not just hear it. In stillness, you begin to feel your way back to this ancient intelligence. You remember that listening is not something you do with the outer ear alone, but with your skin, your breath, your bones.

In that space, your relationship with time shifts. Time is no longer something to fill or conquer. It becomes a teacher. A sculptor. A presence with its own voice. Some truths are given only through long stillness. Some insights need to echo before they land. The pause gives them a place to land. Without it, even the most luminous message will bounce off the surface of a distracted mind.

The sacred pause also interrupts the illusion of control. In the gap between action and reaction, you come face to face with your own compulsions. With the urge to respond, to explain, to grasp. In that gap, you can observe the machinery of your habits. You can feel the weight of your momentum. But you also see the doorway. The opening through which choice can return. The pause breaks the spell. It gives you back to yourself.

In initiatory paths, there is often a moment when the seeker is told to stop. Not to retreat, not to quit, but to become utterly still. These are the moments before thresholds are crossed. The final breath before the veil lifts. The soul is not being denied progress. It is being emptied to receive. Because what comes next is not an extension of the past. It is a rupture. A birth. The pause makes the space for it to emerge.

To truly engage the pause is to surrender to something greater than your personal timeline. It is to trust that wisdom does not always move on your schedule. That revelation is not a commodity to be summoned at will. It arrives in the conditions that honor it. And those conditions are often quiet, unassuming, slow. The pause, then, becomes an act of faith. Not in something outside of you, but in the living intelligence that waits beneath the noise.

This intelligence cannot be rushed. It responds to sincerity, not effort. It is drawn to stillness like flame to air. If you are too full, it will not enter. If you are always speaking, it cannot answer. The pause makes you ready. Not by preparing you with ideas, but by softening your edges. By undoing the urgency. By teaching you to inhabit the space where the unseen becomes knowable.

It is in these spaces that you begin to understand the difference between silence and absence. Silence is presence in its most distilled form. It is the fullness before form. The mind might call it void, but the soul knows it as origin. The source from which words emerge, not the lack of them. When you learn to dwell here, even briefly, your speech changes. Your movement changes. You begin to carry the echo of that stillness with you.

And that is the true power of the pause. It does not simply give you rest. It gives you back your depth. It brings you into alignment with what moves beneath all movement. With what was speaking before you knew how to ask. It teaches you how to live not from constant motion, but from inner rhythm. From listening. From presence. From the sacred intelligence that only reveals itself when you finally become quiet enough to see.

## Dwelling in the Place Between Inhales

*There is a space that most people pass through thousands of times each day without ever noticing. It lives between the inhale and the exhale, where breath pauses not because it is forced to, but because it naturally suspends itself for the briefest moment. That moment is so subtle that the mind rarely lingers there. And yet, it holds a mystery far greater than its duration would suggest.*

---

The pause between breaths is not emptiness. It is a threshold. A space not of action or resistance, but of presence. It is neither the taking in nor the letting go, but the silent holding of both. The body knows this place instinctively. It does not need to be taught how to rest there. It simply needs permission to remember.

Many spiritual traditions have pointed to this space as a portal. Yogic breathwork speaks of *kumbhaka*—the retention of breath—as a gateway to inner stillness. Mystics have found in the breath's rhythm a map to the divine. Not because the breath itself is sacred, but because it reveals something even more essential: that life is not a straight line, but a cycle of receiving, pausing, and releasing. And in the pause, something opens.

This space is not only physiological. It is energetic, emotional, even spiritual. When you bring your awareness into that subtle suspension, you find yourself standing outside of linear time. There is no demand, no rush. It is the absence of urgency. The soft hum beneath the noise. You are not seeking. You are not striving. You are simply here. Fully, quietly, without effort.

And yet, this state is not passive. In fact, it can be deeply generative. The pause between breaths is the womb of intention. It is the moment where what has been meets what is becoming. If you linger there with awareness, even for a few seconds, you begin to feel its intelligence. It is not blank. It is alive. The mind might try to fill it, but the soul recognizes it as a homecoming.

What makes this space powerful is its neutrality. It does not pull you forward or backward. It does not require a story. It simply is. And in that isness, it offers clarity. The kind of clarity that does not come from analysis or effort, but from resonance. The kind that arises when you are no longer reacting, but listening from within.

This space becomes even more vital when you are in moments of uncertainty. In those times, the tendency is to rush toward resolution. To fill the discomfort with plans, explanations, or distractions. But what if the discomfort is not asking to be solved? What if it is asking to be held? The pause between breaths becomes a training ground for this kind of inner holding. It teaches you to dwell in the not-yet, without collapsing into fear. When you begin to cultivate a relationship with this space, your perception of breath changes. You no longer see it as mere physiology. It becomes a guide, a rhythm that reflects the deeper movements of your being. Inhale is expansion. Exhale is release. But the pause is integration. It is the moment your system digests what has just been received, before it lets go and prepares to receive again.

There are teachings that cannot be spoken until the body is quiet enough to hear them. The space between inhales is where those teachings land. Not as thoughts, but as inner shifts. As clarity that feels like still water. You don't explain it. You inhabit it.

It is in that stillness that the illusions of control begin to soften. What felt urgent only moments before loses its grip. The mind, so accustomed to constructing timelines and strategies, slows down enough for a deeper knowing to surface. This knowing does not arrive as a conclusion. It arrives as a felt sense of alignment. A quiet recognition that nothing needs to be rushed, because you are not late. You are in rhythm.

When you allow yourself to rest in this place, you begin to understand the difference between tension and presence. Tension clings. Presence allows. Tension arises from fear, from the resistance to what is. But presence is not interested in resistance. It simply witnesses. It observes without needing to alter. That is the medicine of the pause—it reveals how much of your suffering is born not from life itself, but from the refusal to pause within it.

Even the most transformative experiences begin in silence. Before the insight, there is a moment of suspension. Before the clarity, a brief emptiness. If you fear that emptiness, you fill it too soon, and what could have been a revelation becomes another repetition. But if you remain, if you trust the space to teach you, the pause will begin to show you not just yourself, but the architecture of reality.

In sacred texts, the breath is often associated with spirit. The Hebrew word *ruach*, the Sanskrit *prana*, the Greek *pneuma*—all point to breath as life-force, as animating presence. And yet, none of them define breath as motion alone. The space within the breath is just as holy. It is where spirit dwells before it moves. Where the formless prepares to take form.

The act of dwelling in the pause is not limited to meditation or spiritual practice. It is available in every moment. When you sit with someone you love, and neither of you is speaking, but everything is being said. When you walk into a room and sense that something important is about to happen, but it hasn't yet begun. When you close your eyes at night and feel the gentle border between wakefulness and sleep. These are all pauses. All invitations into the sacred gap.

There is also another kind of pause that life itself sometimes imposes. Illness. Loss. A change you did not ask for. These, too, can become places of profound recalibration if you are willing to listen. Not for answers, but for alignment. The pause doesn't need to explain itself. It simply asks you to be still long enough for your soul to remember what it already knows.

Some of the deepest transformations occur not through force, but through yielding. And yielding does not mean surrendering your power. It means surrendering your resistance to presence. It means letting the breath teach you how to be shaped by something larger than thought. It means trusting that the space between movements is not a void, but a vessel.

Eventually, you begin to feel a shift. Not in your outer circumstances, but in your relationship to them. You stop reacting to life like it's a sequence of problems to solve. You begin to respond from a quieter place. A place that does not rush to fill silence, but allows the silence to reveal what truly matters.

You realize that the breath was never just a function of the body. It was always a messenger. And the message was always the same: everything essential arises from stillness. The pause was not a break from life. It was life, distilled.

And in that realization, you find a kind of freedom. Not the freedom to escape your circumstances, but the freedom to meet them from the still, clear center that lives inside the breath, waiting patiently to be remembered.

# Chapter XI: The Fire That Does Not Burn

## The Flame That Purifies Without Ash

*There is a fire that does not consume. A flame that does not destroy but reveals. In ancient traditions, this flame has been spoken of not as physical, but as spiritual. It burns in the inner sanctum, not to reduce matter to ash, but to release what no longer serves without leaving behind the residue of destruction. It is the flame of consciousness—pure awareness untouched by fear or judgment. When you come into contact with this fire, you are not singed. You are illuminated.*

---

This flame is not born from anger or urgency. It does not rage like a wildfire. It does not punish or seek revenge on what it touches. Instead, it brings a kind of warmth that disarms the defenses, softens the attachments, and dissolves the hardened layers that have calcified around the soul. It purifies not by force, but by truth. And the truth it reveals is not an idea, but a direct encounter with what is real within you.

To meet this flame, you must be willing to let go of your addiction to struggle. Not all growth needs to come through chaos. Not all transformation requires collapse. There is a sacred kind of purification that happens through still presence, through the steady gaze of awareness that neither flinches nor fights. This is what the mystics understood when they described the divine as a refining fire. Not a fire that scars, but one that clarifies.

What gets purified is not the soul itself—the soul is already whole. What burns away are the illusions we've layered over it: the false narratives, the inherited beliefs, the fear-formed identities we wear like armor. These are not who you are. They are the smoke, not the flame. And when the true inner fire touches them, they begin to dissolve, not with drama, but with clarity. The more you allow this to happen, the more your life begins to feel spacious, like something essential has returned.

This kind of purification asks something simple but radical: that you stop identifying with the ashes. That you stop trying to define yourself by what you've outgrown. The stories of suffering, the identities formed around wounds, the patterns you once needed to survive—they may have served a purpose, but they are not your essence. And when the fire begins to rise within you, it's not asking for your pain. It's asking for your presence.

Presence is the fuel of this flame. Not effort. Not striving. Just the willingness to stay with what is true. In that staying, something begins to shift. What once felt heavy starts to lift. Not because you forced it away, but because you finally stopped feeding it your attention. This is the quiet power of the flame that purifies without ash. It teaches you to let go without collapse. To shed without fear. To release without needing to be broken first.

And in this space of inward softening, something else begins to appear. Not the roar of transformation, but the silence that follows it. The stillness that says: you do not need to become someone else to be whole. You do not need to be remade. You only need to be seen. And what the flame sees in you is not brokenness, but brilliance.

That brilliance was never lost, only veiled. Not by malice or error, but by experience. Life wraps the soul in layers for protection at first. But what once protected can become a prison if not released when the time is right. The flame knows when. It does not rush the process. It waits with infinite patience, only rising when you are ready to see what you have hidden from yourself.

There is no violence in this unfolding. The flame moves like breath, like a sacred wind passing through the corridors of memory and self. It carries no judgment. If grief arises, it holds it. If fear surfaces, it meets it with quiet warmth. Its nature is mercy, not force. Its aim is not to dismantle you but to reveal what remains when everything false is surrendered. It burns clean because it is rooted in love, not in correction.

Many resist this flame, not because they don't want to be free, but because they fear what will be left of them without the familiar weight. They ask, "If I let go of this pain, who will I be?" But the flame doesn't ask you to answer that. It simply invites you to discover. It offers a silent reassurance that what remains will not be hollow but sacred. It is not emptiness that is left behind. It is spaciousness. And in that space, you begin to recognize yourself again, not as a sum of your suffering, but as the witness who was never touched by it.

What begins to purify is not only your inner landscape, but your way of seeing. You no longer interpret events solely through the lens of trauma or survival. You no longer scan your environment for validation or threat. You stop reenacting the past in the present. This shift is subtle at first. You notice you are no longer triggered by the same things. You find yourself responding rather than reacting. A quiet dignity emerges. Not one you built to be strong, but one that rises on its own when all performance drops away. This is not the kind of fire that needs to be controlled. It is not dangerous. It is not chaotic. It does not ask you to be brave in the traditional sense. It only asks you to be honest. To be willing to face what is real. To trust that the letting go will not destroy you, but finally introduce you to yourself. The deeper self. The one who has walked with you through every season, silently watching, patiently waiting for your return.

There is great power in this flame because it cannot be manipulated. You cannot fake your way into its presence. You must come bare. Not perfect. Not ready. Just bare. It doesn't care how far you've wandered, how many masks you wear, how long you've clung to pain as proof of identity. It only cares that you're willing now to see something beyond all that.

And when you do, when you stand without armor in that inner fire, something unmistakable happens. You feel not judged but known. Not exposed but held. And the clarity that arises is not cold. It is alive. It does not just cleanse you of illusion, it reminds you why you came here. You did not come to carry your wounds like trophies. You came to remember the inner radiance that was never touched by them.

This is the flame that purifies without ash. It needs no smoke, no spectacle. It is the silent heat of truth meeting the core of your being. Let it rise. Let it see you. Let it show you that what is most sacred in you cannot be burned, only revealed.

## Divine Will vs. Force of Ego

*There is a tension at the center of every spiritual path. It is not the tension between good and evil, nor between success and failure, but between will and willfulness. Between what arises from a deeper alignment with the current of life and what is projected outward from the mind's insistence on control. To walk the path of wisdom, one must learn to distinguish the voice of Divine Will from the force of ego.*

---

Ego, in its simplest form, is not the enemy. It is the structure that allows us to have an individual experience, to navigate the material world, to form identity and choice. But when left unchecked, the ego begins to demand more than it was designed to carry. It attempts to replace the greater intelligence of life with its own narrow goals. It starts to believe that it knows better than the Source from which it came.

This force of ego is subtle. It doesn't always appear as arrogance or pride. Often, it hides behind noble intentions. It whispers that we are being proactive, ambitious, even responsible. But beneath its surface is a tightening. A push. A contraction of energy that attempts to bend life to a personal agenda. This is not creation. It is coercion. And it always carries with it the seed of exhaustion, because it is unsustainable.

Divine Will, by contrast, is not pushy. It does not arrive with noise or urgency. It arises like an inner knowing, still and quiet but unmistakable. It may not always align with what the ego wants in the moment, but it always aligns with what the soul knows to be true. Divine Will speaks not through fear or pressure, but through resonance. When you hear it, you feel more whole. More real. There is a sense of being carried rather than dragged.

This is not to say that Divine Will is passive. It is immensely powerful. But its power is clean. It moves with clarity and precision, not with panic. When a person aligns with it, they become capable of great action, but without the strain that comes from ego-driven striving. The difference is felt in the quality of effort: Divine Will flows through us, ego-force pushes from us.

This is why it is possible to be busy, yet peaceful. Active, yet surrendered. When aligned with Divine Will, even the most demanding tasks feel infused with meaning. Time seems to stretch. Synchronicities occur. Doors open.

This is not magical thinking. It is the natural result of moving in rhythm with what is already true.

The ego resists this because surrender feels like weakness to it. It fears irrelevance. It believes that if it is not in control, nothing will happen. It does not understand that surrender is not inaction. It is union. The merging of our smaller will with the deeper current of intelligence that already holds the map.

The struggle between ego and Divine Will is not a one-time battle, but a daily discernment. It plays out in small choices. In how we speak. In what we pursue. In the pauses between thoughts. It is not just about what we do, but why and how we do it. And this requires honesty. The kind of honesty that strips away performance and asks, "Where is this really coming from?" At first, this can be uncomfortable. The ego will not go quietly. It may reassert itself under new disguises. But over time, if we remain vigilant and humble, the center of gravity begins to shift. We begin to feel the difference between effort that depletes and effort that fulfills. Between noise and signal. Between the force that grasps and the will that guides.

As the center of gravity shifts, we begin to see more clearly where our energy has been leaking. The striving that once felt virtuous begins to look hollow. The noise we took as drive reveals itself as fear wearing ambition as a mask. And the silence we once fled begins to feel like home. In that stillness, Divine Will speaks with increasing clarity, not as instruction from above, but as a movement from within. It becomes less about deciphering some cryptic command and more about allowing the truth to rise through you without interference.

This kind of inner listening requires humility, but not the kind confused with self-erasure. True humility is spacious. It acknowledges the vast intelligence behind existence and allows oneself to become its vessel, not its master. It makes no grand gestures but lives from a quiet alignment. This is not submission in the way the ego fears it. It is the most radical form of participation.

The more one aligns with this rhythm, the less one feels the need to convince others or defend one's path. Divine Will does not need defending. It carries its own authority. When you are in it, your presence alone speaks. Your decisions carry coherence, even when they defy logic. Others may not understand, but those attuned will feel the signal. There is no need to persuade. You are no longer seeking permission.

The force of ego often disguises itself in the pursuit of greatness. It shouts, "I must leave a legacy, I must make an impact." But when you peel back the layers, you often find a wound beneath the performance. A wound that fears being forgotten. A voice that has not yet remembered its origin. Divine Will, on the other hand, leaves behind something far deeper than legacy. It plants seeds in invisible soil. It moves in ways that change timelines, not headlines. It restores order in places others cannot see.

There will still be times when the ego attempts to hijack the journey. It will try to spiritualize its demands, to use the language of truth while serving the old hunger for control. This is why inner discernment must remain sharp. Every day, every moment, you must ask: What is the energy behind this action? What is driving this choice? Is it clean, or is it tainted with personal grasping?

Divine Will is not always comfortable, but it is always true. It may ask you to walk away from what is familiar. It may lead you through uncertainty, without offering the kind of guarantees the ego demands. But it also grants access to a different kind of strength, one that does not burn out or fracture under pressure. A strength born from coherence with the greater pattern.

To live this way is not to abandon responsibility, but to redefine it. Your responsibility is not to uphold the ego's image of success, but to remain faithful to what you are truly here to do. And that may not look grand. It may not be praised. But it will be real. It will carry the weight of something eternal moving through the temporary.

You are not asked to be perfect in this. You are asked to be willing. Willing to notice when you slip into force. Willing to return. Willing to trust the slow intelligence of the soul over the impatient calculations of the mind. You are asked to become a tuning fork for truth. A place where Divine Will can sound its note into the world without distortion.

And when you do, your life becomes an offering. Not a monument to self, but a bridge between what is unseen and what longs to be made visible. You no longer chase meaning. You become the place where meaning appears. This is not the result of achievement, but of alignment. And it is here, in this quiet revolution, that the ego finally bows. Not in defeat, but in recognition. It was never meant to lead. It was always meant to serve.

# Holding Power Without Consuming

*To hold power without consuming is to stand in the current of energy without needing to devour it. It is not the grasping of the hungry, nor the performance of the dominant. It is the sacred capacity to let energy move through you without becoming addicted to its intensity or drunk on its influence.*

---

In most of the modern world, power is misunderstood as possession. People strive to accumulate it, to own it, to display it. Whether it is financial, physical, social, or spiritual, power is often pursued for how it can elevate the self-image. But when power is pursued in this way, it begins to corrode. The more it is hoarded, the more it distorts. The more it is consumed, the more it consumes in return.

True power is not taken. It is carried. It is a living current, not a fixed possession. You do not need to conquer others to access it. You need to become a vessel refined enough to hold it without distortion. And this requires a kind of inner purity, not in a moralistic sense, but in an energetic one. You must not seek to use it for the satisfaction of lack.

If you hold power with clean hands, it amplifies what is already true. It becomes a luminous force that brings clarity, direction, and coherence. But if you grasp power with unresolved wounds, it will magnify those too. The more forcefully you try to wield it, the more it slips through your fingers, or worse, turns against you. This is why the ancient teachings emphasized self-mastery before external mastery. Not as control, but as containment.

To contain power is not to suppress it, but to allow it to remain whole within you. To not leak it into seduction, manipulation, or overextension. To not let it become currency for validation. This is the path of spiritual adulthood. It is not flashy. It does not always look impressive. But it creates an unshakable integrity.

Many who awaken to inner energy or hidden knowledge feel the temptation to use it as leverage. Even subtle insights can become tools of hierarchy if the ego co-opts them. The danger is not in the power itself, but in the hunger to be seen as powerful. This is a shadow that wears robes, speaks in sacred language, and hides behind virtue. It consumes in the name of light.

When you truly hold power without consuming, you do not need recognition. You do not need to dominate a room or win an argument. Your presence speaks more than your words. Others may not understand why they feel different around you, but they do. There is something grounded, still, and vast in you that cannot be faked.

This power does not depend on external status. It arises from alignment, not accumulation. You can be wealthy or not, visible or hidden, leading or supporting. None of that affects the essence of it. Because it is not about role. It is about resonance. And the clearer your frequency, the more power flows without effort or demand.

The true holders of power are often the least interested in appearing powerful. They do not seek attention. They do not seek control. They simply become trustworthy vessels. And because they do not consume what passes through them, they are entrusted with more. Not in volume, but in quality. The kind of power that can shape timelines without lifting a hand.

The more refined your relationship with power becomes, the more subtle the temptations are. They no longer shout through obvious ambition. Instead, they whisper through the desire to be appreciated for your restraint, or to be seen as above it all. These temptations are not always driven by malice but by the lingering remnants of identity seeking reinforcement. Even the image of being humble can become a structure of ego.

To hold power without consuming also means letting go of the story that it is yours. Nothing that flows through you is truly yours. It is entrusted to you for a time, a purpose, a passage. When you forget this, you begin to grasp. And when you grasp, you contract. The current slows. The clarity fades. The integrity wavers.

The initiates of many ancient paths were trained not to awaken power first, but to purify the vessel. Not out of superstition, but out of precision. Power follows purity not as a reward but as a natural alignment. When your motives are clean, the energy you carry does not need to be managed or protected. It flows cleanly because there is no interference. You do not need to defend it, because you are not holding it for yourself.

There is a stillness in those who carry power in this way. It is not passive, but undisturbed. It allows them to act from clarity rather than urgency. They do not move because they are triggered or challenged. They move when the moment calls, and they do so with exactness. Their words cut through illusion not by volume, but by alignment.

To become such a vessel requires a discipline that is not driven by pressure. It is the discipline of integrity. You are not trying to be good. You are remaining clear. And that clarity becomes its own guidance. You begin to notice the subtle signs of corruption long before they become action. A tightness in the chest. A desire to impress. A flicker of wanting to prove something. These are not to be judged, only seen. Witnessed, acknowledged, and released.

One of the greatest tests of holding power is what you do when no one is watching. When there is no applause to earn and no structure to enforce your ethics. When power could be used without consequence. In that space, you meet the truth of your alignment. Do you still serve what is greater than you, even in silence? Do you still choose the path that preserves the field rather than feeds your image?

Holding power without consuming is not about perfection. It is about continual refinement. There will be moments when you misstep, moments when your own shadow surprises you. But the key is what you do with those moments. Do you justify them, or do you transmute them? Do you hide them, or do you allow them to teach you?

This path is quiet. It does not often win the approval of crowds. It does not guarantee recognition or safety. But it births something far more lasting. It births a kind of power that does not collapse when challenged, because it is not built on illusion. It does not fluctuate with opinion, because it is not rooted in performance. It is the kind of power that holds space for transformation simply by existing.

In the end, to hold power without consuming is to know that you are not the source. You are the instrument. And your refinement is the offering. The cleaner you become, the more sacred the current that moves through you. Not for your sake, but for the sake of the world that is shaped by what you carry. You do not need to shine to be luminous. You only need to stay true.

# Chapter XII: The Veil of the Infinite Faces

## The Reflections That Are Not You

*A mirror reflects what is shown to it. It does not evaluate, it does not distinguish essence from surface. It simply offers back a likeness, shaped by proximity and light. Much of what you believe to be "you" has been formed in these mirrors: the glances of others, the expectations of culture, the silent agreements made in childhood. These reflections feel real because they are repeated. And repetition, in the absence of discernment, becomes identity. But the spiritual path calls you to something different. It asks not just that you look within, but that you learn to see what is not yours. Not all thoughts are yours. Not all stories that feel familiar belong to your essence. Not every emotional imprint is part of your core. You are not required to carry what was projected onto you.*

---

From a young age, you absorbed impressions like wet clay. The tone of a parent's voice, the invisible tension in a room, the way others responded to your light or your silence. These early encounters became mirrors through which you learned what was acceptable, what was safe, what was loved. And in doing so, you began to shape yourself accordingly. Not out of weakness, but out of intelligence. The body and psyche adapt for survival. The child bends to belong. But what bends can harden, and what hardens can be mistaken for truth.

To awaken is to begin the slow, courageous process of distinguishing between your core essence and the impressions left on its surface. This is not about rejecting the world. It is about reclaiming the original signal beneath the noise. It is about learning to differentiate between the pulse of your soul and the echoes of other people's fear.

Not all reflections are malicious. Some are even well-intentioned. But a mirror cannot show what lies behind it. You may be praised for traits that are not your deepest gifts, and criticized for aspects that are misunderstood. If you build your identity on the responses of others, you risk becoming a collage of impressions, stitched together by survival and validation. You risk mistaking familiarity for truth.

This distortion does not only come from individuals. It is embedded in systems, beliefs, and roles. There are reflections offered by institutions, traditions, even spiritual communities. You may be encouraged to perform certain virtues, adopt certain language, follow certain codes. Some of these may align with your path. Others may gently steer you away from yourself, until you are living someone else's version of awakening.

Discernment is a sacred task. It does not come from rejection, but from stillness. The more deeply you listen, the more clearly you feel the dissonance when something is not yours. You notice the slight constriction in the chest, the vague numbness, the need to explain yourself. These are not flaws. They are signals. They tell you when you are operating in someone else's mirror, rather than your own source.

There is great freedom in realizing you do not need to correct every false reflection. You do not need to argue with distortion. You only need to remain faithful to your alignment. The more you embody your true frequency, the more false reflections dissolve on their own. They lose their grip, not through conflict, but through clarity.

There is no need to dismantle every illusion. The most lasting transformation does not come from dissecting what is false, but from embodying what is real. When you stand rooted in what arises from within—before it is shaped by opinion or comparison—your presence begins to untangle the web without effort. There is a deeper intelligence in truth that does the work for you. You don't need to explain why something no longer fits. You only need to stop wearing it.

But to reach this clarity, you must become intimate with the mechanics of distortion. Not intellectually, but energetically. You must feel how certain words tighten your breath, how certain dynamics dim your radiance. You must notice which interactions leave you confused, fragmented, depleted. These are not failures in communication. They are moments where the mirror reflects a distortion that does not belong to your frequency. And if you confuse the mirror for the self, you will spend your life polishing someone else's surface.

Many carry burdens they were never meant to bear. Guilt inherited from generations. Shame wrapped around their gifts. Pressure to fulfill roles they never agreed to. These burdens do not always come loudly. Sometimes they come through subtle reflections: the disappointed glance, the unmet expectation, the unspoken rule. Over time, these impressions are internalized as self-concepts. The ego adopts them in order to survive, and then defends them as identity.

To break this spell, presence is not enough. You must enter a deeper level of listening—one that is not reactive but reverent. You begin to ask, not just what you feel, but where it comes from. You observe which parts of you feel authentic, and which parts feel rehearsed. You begin to notice when a reaction is arising from past defense rather than present clarity. You begin to trust the voice that arises in silence, not the one that trembles under scrutiny.

There is no need to rush this unraveling. The shedding of false reflections is not a war. It is a gentle, luminous remembering. It may be disorienting at times, because identity often offers structure, even when it is based on illusion. But there is a deeper structure beneath it—one built not on image, but on essence. When you stop trying to maintain the reflection, you begin to feel the truth that does not require mirrors at all.

In that space, what is yours begins to return. The tone of your voice shifts. The rhythm of your choices changes. You begin to move from a different axis. Not to be seen, not to be approved of, but because something ancient and pure is guiding you again. You begin to recognize when something resonates, not because it is familiar, but because it is aligned.

And with time, you see others differently too. You no longer chase their approval, nor resent their misunderstanding. You see their reflections as their own mirrors in motion—nothing to cling to, nothing to fear. You begin to relate from essence to essence, not role to role. You meet others not through your armor, but through your quiet knowing. There is less need to perform. More space to simply be.

This is the turning point: when identity becomes less about how you are seen and more about how you feel in your own presence. When your choices are no longer shaped by distortion, but by resonance. When the inner compass becomes stronger than any reflection. This is what it means to come home to yourself.

You are not the reflection. You are the source of light that makes the mirror possible. And once you remember that, nothing that is not you can hold power over you again.

# The Game of Names and Forms

*There is a peculiar comfort in naming things. A certain solidity takes hold once something has a label, a category, a defined role. The unknown becomes bearable when it is given a name. But names are not reality. They are approximations, placeholders, constructs designed to stabilize what is essentially fluid. Language carves boundaries into a world that, in its raw state, knows no borders. Forms emerge from this naming, but behind the form is movement. Behind the movement, essence.*

---

Children understand this before they are taught otherwise. They see with the eyes of immediacy, touching life without layering it with concepts. A tree is not a "tree" until the word is taught. Before that, it is color, texture, being. It is not separate from the child. It is part of the same field of wonder. Once the name arrives, the boundary is drawn. The tree becomes "object," the child becomes "subject," and the seamless field is divided into parts.

This game of names and forms is not inherently wrong. It is the architecture of culture, the tool through which civilizations are built. But when we forget it is a game, when we believe the label is the thing itself, we lose touch with the living essence behind the structure. The map becomes the territory. The symbol replaces the experience. And the sacred is reduced to a concept recited rather than a presence felt.

Spirituality itself is not exempt from this game. The names of deities, the forms of rituals, the doctrines and dogmas—all are structures built atop a mystery that cannot be fully captured. They are meant to point toward the ineffable, not contain it. But the mind grows attached to structure. It seeks to own the divine by naming it. And in doing so, it often closes the door it meant to open.

This is why traditions often speak of the hidden name, the true name, the name that is not spoken. Not because secrecy is inherently sacred, but because the unspeakable cannot be reduced to syllables. The real cannot be captured by sound alone. What is eternal resists definition, not out of rebellion, but because it is always more than the container built to hold it.

In ancient metaphysical texts, there is often the idea that the act of naming is also the act of limiting. To name is to define, and to define is to confine. This is not always a problem. We need limits to operate in the visible world.

But if we begin to confuse the structure with the source, we lose the thread. We mistake the robe for the priest, the script for the truth, the form for the essence.

The ego thrives in the realm of names. It builds identity through labels: I am this, not that. I do this, not that. I follow this path, not that one. These identifications help form a sense of self, but they also create separation. When held too tightly, they become prisons. They turn living beings into roles, expressions of life into categories, and divine mystery into religious branding.

Letting go of the grip on names does not mean abandoning language. It means remembering its place. Language is a tool, not a truth. Forms are expressions, not absolutes. You can bow before a sacred statue and recognize the formless presence it represents, without believing that the stone itself holds the whole of the divine. You can speak of love, yet know the word will always fall short of the fire it attempts to describe.

When names are held lightly, they become bridges instead of walls. A symbol that is not clung to can open a door. A tradition that is honored without rigidity can serve as a vessel rather than a cage. What matters is not the form itself, but the consciousness with which it is held. A name becomes sacred only when it is animated by presence. Without that, it is just sound.

This is the essence of sacred play. In some mystical paths, the universe itself is seen as lila, a divine game, where the Absolute cloaks itself in names and forms, not to forget, but to explore. Every being, every object, every story is a mask worn by the Unnameable. From this view, the spiritual task is not to deny the game, but to remember it is a game. To engage it with full attention while never mistaking it for the final truth.

The soul is not trying to escape form. It is trying to remember itself within form. When you see the dance behind the dancer, the light behind the face, the silence beneath the voice, you begin to shift from identification to awareness. You are not merely your name, your role, your background. These are garments you wear in this lifetime, threads woven into your temporary tapestry. They are not the totality of your being.

What begins to emerge from this shift is a quiet humility. The more deeply you touch the formless, the less need you have to defend the form. You no longer need to convince others of your path, or prove your worth through your roles. You can honor the path you walk while allowing space for other paths. You can stand firm in what speaks to your soul, without needing the world to echo it.

There is power in this loosening. It allows you to move fluidly, to listen more deeply, to release the tension of being right. When you no longer grip the mask as your identity, you become more available to what moves through the mask. You become a clearer vessel. Wisdom is able to pour in because there is space. Life begins to speak, not through the rigid voice of concept, but through the subtle language of being.

You may notice this shift in simple moments. A conversation that no longer requires defense. A prayer that feels less like petition and more like communion. A sense that you are watching yourself act, yet also deeply inhabiting the act. The game is still unfolding, but you are no longer lost in it. You are aware of the player, and of the Source from which the player arises.

Eventually, this recognition becomes less an insight and more a way of being. The name still exists. The form still moves. But you carry an awareness that rests beyond both. The tree is no longer just bark and leaves. It is a pulse. The person across from you is no longer just a name or title. They are an echo of the same silence that breathes through you.

This shift does not remove you from the world. It invites you deeper into it. Fully engaged, fully present, yet unattached to the illusions that once defined your sense of self. The game continues, but the stakes have changed. What once felt like a battle for identity becomes a celebration of essence. And in that space, life begins to reveal its deeper script, one written not in words, but in the rhythm beneath them.

# Removing the Final Mask

*There comes a moment on the path when all the names have been questioned, all the roles gently laid down, all the illusions pierced one by one. The seeker has turned away from the voices of the world, then from the echoes within their own mind, and even from the comfort of their own beliefs. What remains is not a new role or identity to embrace, but the invitation to remove the final mask.*

---

This mask is subtle. It is not a persona worn in front of others, nor a label assigned by society. It is the idea of oneself as a seeker, a spiritual being, a knower of truth. It is the mask that still clings to identity even while proclaiming to transcend it. It may appear refined, even noble, but it still whispers "I." I am the awakened one. I am the one who understands. I am the one who has gone beyond.

This final mask is the most persistent. It lingers because it feels spiritual. Because it is wrapped in silence instead of noise. Because it does not look like pride, but purpose. And yet, it is still a veil. It is still separation. It is still an idea of self.

To remove it is not an act of force, but of surrender. Not the dramatic collapse of a persona, but the quiet relinquishment of even the need to know who you are. It is the moment when the desire to be someone — even someone spiritual, someone free — dissolves in the recognition that what you are cannot be held in the mind.

This is not annihilation, though it may feel like death to the ego. It is the dissolving of all effort to define, control, or possess one's being. It is not becoming nothing, but recognizing that you have always been the field in which all somethings arise. There is no longer a center from which you operate. No self-image to protect. No story to continue.

Paradoxically, this does not lead to emptiness but to a vast aliveness. Without the mask, there is no filter between you and the Real. You meet the world as it is, not as it reflects you back to yourself. You no longer live in the echo of who you think you are, but in the stillness that precedes every echo. Awareness becomes unbound, no longer confined to a shape or story. What arises from here is a sacred ordinariness. There is nothing left to perform. Nothing left to achieve. You breathe, walk, speak, laugh, weep, and none of it is about becoming someone. You are simply present. And in that presence, the radiance of the formless begins to shine through every form. You are not trying to embody truth. You are not trying to awaken. You are not trying to purify. All effort falls away, and what remains is a clarity so intimate it has no name.

This clarity is not passive. It is not resignation. It is alert, awake, deeply attuned. But it no longer originates from identity. It is not concerned with progress. It moves as needed, speaks when moved to, remains still when silence is true. There is no agenda behind it. No hunger for recognition or control.

Even spiritual insight becomes just another wave in the ocean. It arises, it passes, and it does not attach. You do not build a home around it or place it on an altar. You do not gather others around your light. You simply live, and your life begins to speak the truth more clearly than any doctrine could. The moment this shift stabilizes, you stop seeking mirrors. You are not interested in reflection, comparison, or spiritual validation. Not because you reject others, but because you no longer need to see yourself through them. The final mask falls quietly, and with it, the last illusion of separation.

You become transparent to yourself. There is no more tension in the being, no background noise of self-maintenance. What once consumed energy — protecting an image, defending a path, maintaining a spiritual identity — is simply no longer there. You do not wake up each morning needing to return to yourself. You are already here. And in that presence, everything is permitted to arise and pass without clinging or resistance.

Emotions continue to appear. Thoughts continue to move. The body remains sensitive to the world. But there is no longer an inner commentator assigning meaning, judging, or trying to sculpt experience into something safer, higher, or more spiritual. Life is met without contraction. Sorrow can pass through like wind. Joy can bloom without need to grasp. Silence can envelop everything without becoming a goal. Even the old patterns of mind may surface, but they no longer define the space in which they appear. You are not interested in managing them. You are not interested in fixing the echo of what you no longer believe to be you.

This is not spiritual bypassing. It is not indifference. It is the end of personalization. The river flows, and you do not mistake the ripples for identity. What you once called "my pain" or "my insight" is now just sensation, just energy, just movement through the field of awareness. And this field is not owned. It does not belong to a character or a name. It is shared, ungraspable, luminous.

In this condition, compassion arises not from virtue, but from recognition. You see the struggle of others and you remember. You see the masks they wear and you remember. But you do not try to rip them away. You do not impose silence. You do not convert. You do not preach. You become a gentle mirror, not reflecting identity, but reflecting what lies behind it. Your presence becomes a kind of permission for others to release their own masks, but only when they are ready. There is no rush, no mission. Only the quiet transmission of what is.

To live like this is to dwell in radical simplicity. Not in poverty or renunciation necessarily, but in freedom from entanglement. You do not fear success or failure because neither touches what you are. You do not depend on rituals or structures to keep you aligned. If they serve, they are used. If they fall away, nothing is lost. You are not centered in the form, but in the formless that gives rise to all forms.

This inner stillness is not about retreating from the world, but seeing through it. You can walk among cities or forests, speak to strangers or remain silent, create or rest, all from the same centerless clarity. Your life is no longer about becoming something. It is about revealing what has never been absent. The final mask is not replaced with a new one. It is left on the ground, like a shell that has served its purpose.

Eventually, even the notion of awakening dissolves. You are not aware of being enlightened. You are not aware of holding knowledge. You are not measuring how awake you are. That entire framework collapses. You simply are. And in that, there is a fullness so total it needs no name.

The final mask is not torn away in drama. It is not removed through effort. It falls when you no longer need to be anything at all. Not the wise one. Not the student. Not even the witness. Just presence, unguarded, unmoved, and utterly open.

This is the return. Not to who you were before the world shaped you, but to what was never shaped. The flame before the candle. The breath before the first word. The truth that waits behind every form. You are not trying to find it anymore. You are it. And now, you live accordingly.

# Chapter XIII: The Throne in the Cave of the Heart

## Silence as Supreme Teacher

*There is a wisdom that speaks without sound, a transmission that bypasses language altogether. This wisdom does not explain, convince, or argue. It does not dazzle with rhetoric or wrap itself in complex frameworks. It waits in stillness. And only those who know how to enter that stillness will hear it.*

Silence is not merely the absence of noise. It is a presence, alive and complete. When we approach it with reverence, we begin to recognize that it is not empty but full — not passive but immensely intelligent. It carries a depth that no doctrine can reach, and an intimacy that no spoken truth can match.

The ancient mystics knew this. Before sacred texts were written, teachings were whispered into the silence between two beings sitting in recognition. The greatest initiations happened in the hush after the question, not in the answer itself. In the pauses of prayer, the spaces between chants, the quiet just before a vision — this is where truth emerges without shape, yet clearer than any form.

To allow silence to teach is to undergo a reversal of the conditioned mind. The intellect has been trained to seek meaning through addition: more concepts, more data, more articulation. But silence works by subtraction. It removes what is not essential. It does not feed your identity, it strips it. And in the removal, it reveals.

When you sit in true silence — not performing stillness, not imagining a serene state, but genuinely resting without agenda — something begins to soften. The layers of thought unravel. The body no longer postures itself to be seen. The breath quiets. And what remains is a raw, undistorted awareness that knows what is real because it no longer needs to define it.

This is why silence cannot be taught like other subjects. It cannot be dissected or systematized. It must be entered. It must be met. And the moment you try to master it, you lose it. It requires your surrender, not your skill.

In silence, there are no affirmations, no goals, no spiritual performance. There is only the unadorned presence of being. This presence holds you without commentary, without judgment, and without the need for progress. It does not ask you to become anything. It only asks that you stop running from what you already are.

And in this resting, the mind begins to experience its own quiet nature. Thoughts may still arise, but they are no longer fed. They pass like clouds over a sky that no longer clings. Feelings may still stir, but they are no longer mistaken for the self. Silence shows you that there is a space deeper than thought and more stable than emotion, and it is within this space that real knowing begins to take form.

This knowing is not intellectual. It does not offer explanation, yet it clarifies. It does not promise certainty, yet it stabilizes. It comes not through effort, but through intimacy. The more you trust it, the more it reveals. The more you allow it, the more it shapes your life from within.

Let the silence have the last word. Not because you have given up, but because you have realized that the voice you were waiting to hear was not external. It was never above you or beyond you. It was always beneath the noise, behind the striving, inside the breathless longing for something more. And here, in this moment of recognition, the student stops asking and begins to listen.

The listening that arises in silence is not passive. It is alert, present, deeply attuned. It listens not only to sound but to the quality of being beneath all appearances. It hears the truth in what is not said, in what cannot be put into language. It senses alignment, incongruence, inner resistance, and openness — not because it is analyzing, but because it is empty enough to feel.

This is why silence becomes the supreme teacher. It shows you what is real without pointing to it. It reveals where you are attached, where you grasp, where you still seek to control. It mirrors your discomfort when you want to escape. It shows you how restless your mind has become. And yet it never condemns you. It simply waits until you are ready to stop escaping.

The great paradox is that silence contains everything. When the surface noise is stripped away, what remains is the entire cosmos within you. The patterns of your soul, the impulses of your being, the forgotten threads of clarity — all of these begin to speak when the shouting of the world is no longer louder than your own presence.

It is in silence that you begin to notice what is guiding you. Not a voice, not a command, but a knowing. This knowing does not rise from fear. It is not driven by ambition or identity. It does not speak in urgent tones. It is still. And in that stillness, it carries authority. Not the authority of control, but of truth that needs no justification.

You begin to realize that this truth does not argue with illusion. It does not engage in debates with the ego. It does not demand allegiance. It simply exists. And its existence is invitation enough.

Silence reorients you from surface to source. It shifts the center of gravity from doing to being. From concept to essence. And the more you dwell in it, the more you are taught not by accumulation, but by recognition. You remember what has always been within you, waiting to be seen again.

It is not an easy path. Silence is often avoided because it dismantles illusion. It brings up everything you have buried, ignored, or distracted yourself from. It strips away the stories. It leaves you naked. And yet, it is in this very nakedness that you become available to the sacred.

You will be tempted to fill the space again. To speak prematurely, to interpret, to reach for meaning before it lands. But if you can stay — if you can hold the quiet a little longer — something begins to open. A clarity that was not summoned. A peace that does not depend on circumstances. A truth that does not seek validation.

Let it teach you. Let it undo you. Let it show you how much of your life has been built on noise. Let it reveal that your strength is not in how much you say, but in how deeply you can be without saying anything at all.

And when the time does come to speak, you will speak from a different place. Not from reaction or defense, not from the need to prove, but from alignment. Your words will be fewer, but they will carry weight. Not because they are clever, but because they are clean. They will emerge from the same stillness that once held you, and they will carry its fragrance.

In the end, silence is not a technique or a practice. It is a return. A return to what has never changed, even as everything else moved. A return to the center that watches the world rise and fall without being shaken.

To walk with silence is to walk with the source. To trust it is to become intimate with truth. To dwell in it is to remember who you are before the world taught you to forget. And in that remembrance, everything begins anew — not louder, not brighter, but deeper. More real. More whole.

# The Unshakable Center

*There is a point within you that does not move. It is not touched by mood, by memory, or by the ever-shifting tides of life. It is not shaped by success or shattered by failure. It neither inflates with praise nor contracts under criticism. This point — still, sovereign, and silent — is your unshakable center.*

---

You may have forgotten it. You may have spent most of your life circling around it without knowing it was there, chasing experiences that come and go, investing identity in thoughts that rise and fall. But the center has never left. It waits in perfect stillness beneath the surface storm, like the eye of a hurricane that remains unmoved as the winds rage.

To know this center is not to withdraw from the world. It is to engage with it differently. When you live from the center, you begin to see things as they are, rather than through the distortions of fear or desire. You act from clarity, not compulsion. You move not to prove, but because something within you aligns with the movement. This shift does not make you passive. It makes you precise.

The unshakable center is not a construct. It is not built by effort. It cannot be reached by stacking affirmations or mental frameworks. In fact, it often reveals itself when everything you thought made you strong begins to fall away. You may first glimpse it in moments of crisis, when your usual strategies collapse, and you discover there is something in you that does not collapse with them.

Or you may find it in the quiet spaces — in meditation, in deep presence, in those brief moments when thought ceases and what remains is simply awareness itself. That awareness is not separate from the center. It is the center, recognized. It does not need a name. It does not ask for recognition. It is the root of who you are.

Many traditions have spoken of it in different ways. The Tao. Atman. The Self. The Witness. The Still Point. But words point only vaguely. What matters is the direct contact. And that contact is not a matter of belief. It is a matter of remembrance.

To live without contact with this center is to live in reactivity. It is to become a puppet of outer conditions. You are kind when people are kind, defensive when attacked, elated when praised, crushed when rejected. You are at the mercy of everything because you are anchored in nothing. And so life feels unstable, unpredictable, threatening.

But when you return to the center, something reverses. You stop sourcing your identity from what happens to you. You begin to experience what moves around you without losing your grounding in what is within you. You watch the waves, but you are no longer drowning in them.

This does not mean you become cold or detached. It means you begin to live with a different kind of warmth — one that is not burned by emotion, but guided by inner alignment. You feel, but you are not ruled by feeling. You care, but you do not cling. You act, but you are not entangled.

This shift is not a one-time event. It is a returning. Again and again, you are invited back to the center — through disruption, through beauty, through silence, through pain. Each moment becomes a doorway. But the choice to step through is always yours.

The next time you feel pulled into reaction, pause. Not to analyze, not to suppress, but to remember. Ask yourself: from where am I moving? Is it from the noise on the surface, or from the quiet that knows? And in that pause, you might feel it — the gravity of the center pulling you back.

The more often you return to that pause, the more familiar the stillness becomes. What at first feels like emptiness begins to reveal a quiet richness. You notice that it is not lacking anything. It does not strive, does not chase, does not compare. And yet, from it arises the most authentic expression of your being. You begin to see that silence is not absence, but presence in its purest form.

This is not a state you need to maintain through willpower. The very idea of controlling it takes you away from it. The center does not need to be held. It holds you. The moment you stop resisting life's movement or grasping for stability in external structures, it becomes apparent again, like a current beneath the surface. The practice is not about fabrication, but about uncovering what has always been.

And from this place, discernment sharpens. You begin to feel the difference between what is arising from truth and what is generated by fear. You begin to sense when something is aligned and when it is forced. No longer driven by urgency or the need to prove, you become deeply selective with your energy. You stop scattering your attention and instead move with deliberate clarity. This is the essence of spiritual maturity: not withdrawal from life, but movement with precision and presence.

You may still encounter chaos. You will still feel sorrow, anger, frustration. These do not vanish. But they do not own you. You allow them to move through, without becoming them. You can witness their arrival, learn from their presence, and let them go when their message is complete. Because you are not the storm. You are the sky that holds it.

Even in the face of pressure, you remain rooted. Others may misunderstand you, challenge you, provoke you. But when you no longer need external validation, when your sense of self is no longer tethered to appearance, the opinions of others lose their power. You are not hardened by this. You are freed.

There is a paradox here. From this inner stability, creativity flourishes. Spontaneity becomes natural. Because you are not operating from tension, your actions are infused with effortless energy. You speak what is needed, do what is true, and then return to stillness. There is no drama in it. There is no performance. There is simply congruence.

This center is not separate from divinity. In fact, it is the doorway through which the sacred enters your life. It is the space in which the timeless whispers. It is where your will and higher will begin to move as one. When you act from this center, you do not push. You are carried. When you speak from it, words come with resonance. When you listen from it, you hear more than sound.

And yet, the ego will try to reassert itself. It will create distractions. It will tell you there is something to fix, something to chase, something to fear. It will pull you toward familiar loops of reaction. This, too, is part of the path. Not to be fought, but to be recognized. Each pull away is another invitation to return. Each forgetting is an opportunity to remember.

Over time, this remembering becomes less effortful. It becomes a gravitational pull. The more you rest in the center, the more you recognize that nothing essential has ever been missing. You are not building wholeness. You are uncovering it. And the world begins to reflect that wholeness back to you, not always in comfort, but in clarity.

Let the world move as it does. Let others have their tides. Your task is not to still the ocean, but to find your anchor within it. And from that place, to live with openness, steadiness, and truth.

This is the return to the unshakable center. Not an escape, but a remembering. Not a retreat, but a revelation. Not a concept, but a lived knowing.

And from here, life is no longer something to survive or conquer. It becomes something you embody, with both grace and strength.

## Ruling Without Reaching

*There is a power that does not clench. A presence that does not grasp. It governs not through domination, persuasion, or demand, but through alignment. This is the essence of ruling without reaching. It is a quiet authority that arises not from effort, but from the unshakable integrity of being.*

In most worldly models of power, reaching is glorified. You are told to chase, to strive, to climb, to seize. Success is measured by how much ground you cover, how many things you collect, how quickly you achieve. This kind of reaching, though often admired, is deeply agitated. It springs from an inner belief that something essential is still missing. And so, one reaches not because of fullness, but because of lack.

But there is another way of holding power. It does not stretch toward the future or grasp at outcomes. It does not seek to manipulate appearances. Instead, it draws reality into coherence by the force of its own settled presence. You become the tuning fork. You no longer push to be heard. The resonance of your clarity begins to do the work for you.

To rule without reaching is not passivity. It is precision. It is mastery over the inner compulsion to prove, perform, or control. It is the ability to act without chasing, to move without leaning forward. And paradoxically, it makes you far more impactful. Because you are not diluted by craving, your energy becomes potent. You become the still point in a room full of motion. This quality is deeply magnetic. People sense when someone does not need to dominate to lead, does not need to reach in order to rule. It disarms the patterns of power that rely on fear or intimidation. It awakens a different kind of respect. Not one born of status, but of felt stability.

This form of sovereignty requires deep self-knowledge. You must be able to sense when your desire is no longer clean. You must catch yourself when your action is subtly laced with fear of being overlooked, forgotten, or unseen. It means pausing when your instinct is to grasp. Not to suppress yourself, but to listen beneath the impulse. What part of you believes that something must be added to your being in order for it to be enough?

Often, the one who reaches the most is the one who feels least rooted. They reach because they feel like they are not already in possession of what matters. But when you begin to recognize the sacred within you, when you live from that deep root, the compulsion to reach loses its grip. You do not have to pursue what is already yours by nature. Your very presence begins to call it in.

This is not about collapsing into inaction. It is not about detaching from life or its responsibilities. It is about a different posture. You move, but from fullness, not from fear. You speak, but without needing to be louder than others. You choose, but not because you are trying to control the field. You become like the sun. It does not reach. It radiates.

To come to this level of presence, one must walk through many layers of undoing. The ego thrives on reaching. It convinces you that without reaching, you will disappear. That if you do not keep striving, someone else will take your place. This fear is subtle but persistent. And so, most people spend their entire lives reaching, never realizing that they are running in circles around their own throne.

When all striving dissolves, what often remains is a quiet, steady clarity. This clarity is not dramatic. It does not announce itself. It does not seek validation. Yet it has the weight of something real. In this state, your presence becomes a beacon rather than a tool. It stops being something you use to get results and instead becomes the very force that reshapes the space around you.

This kind of presence does not require you to be impressive. It asks only that you be true. The more you empty yourself of distortion, the more you become a vessel for something greater than personality. People can feel the difference. There is a stillness in you that is not absent, but deeply alive. You begin to hold power not because you take it, but because you are no longer fragmented. Your coherence becomes your crown.

In spiritual traditions, the most powerful masters rarely shout. Their words are few. Their actions minimal. But when they do speak, everything quiets. This is not a product of performance. It comes from the purity of alignment. From the years of inner refinement that made them unable to act from distortion. They have nothing left to prove. Because of this, they can command without command. Influence without pressure. Rule without reach.

There is a sacred paradox in this. The moment you stop needing power, you begin to embody it. The moment you no longer seek influence, your very being becomes influential. This does not mean retreating into passivity or becoming invisible. It means that you step out of the false game entirely. You do not compete. You do not chase. You stand.

From that place, action flows with precision. You no longer act out of compulsion. You wait for timing that is real, not rushed. You learn to discern between movement that is aligned and movement that is noisy. The quality of your doing changes because it no longer arises from a sense of lack. Even your silence becomes a form of participation. Not withdrawal, but deep listening.

There is a sovereignty that cannot be taken or given. It comes not from others' recognition but from the full inhabiting of your own soul. When you carry this kind of sovereignty, your leadership becomes subtle but undeniable. You may not lead with title, status, or strategy. You lead by your frequency. And that frequency is shaped not by how much you reach, but by how fully you rest in what is already whole within you.

To live this way requires vigilance. The pull to reach can return in disguise. It may appear as ambition, generosity, urgency, or even purpose. But underneath, if you are honest, you will often find a trace of fear. Fear that being is not enough. Fear that you will be forgotten if you do not remind the world of your importance. Fear that if you do not control the outcome, you will not be safe.

To break free from this cycle is not to deny the desire to serve or express. It is to cleanse that desire of distortion. To act not from deficiency, but from inner abundance. To give because you are overflowing, not because you are trying to be seen. To lead because you are rooted, not because you are trying to compensate for an unseen wound.

You do not become less effective when you stop reaching. You become more precise. More trusted. More powerful. Not in the way the world often measures power, but in the way that reshapes lives at their center. People begin to feel different in your presence. Not because you have overwhelmed them, but because you have reminded them of something they forgot in themselves. That they too can stop reaching. That they too can be still and powerful at once.

This is the invitation. Not to abandon action, but to purify its source. To remember that your greatest influence comes not from how much noise you make, but from how deeply you inhabit the truth. To rule not by stretching beyond yourself, but by standing fully within the ground of what you already are.

## The Transmission That Requires No Tongue

*There is a language older than words. A teaching that does not travel through sound, syllables, or letters. It moves directly into the receptive mind, into the subtle body, into the silent core of being. It requires no tongue because it is not delivered through speech. It requires no ears because it is not heard. It is felt. It is known. It is transmitted by presence.*

---

This transmission is ancient, predating civilizations and scriptures. It exists in the gaze of a master, in the alignment of one who has seen beyond form, in the stillness of a moment when nothing is spoken but everything is understood. The receiver does not analyze it, translate it, or attempt to name it. They simply meet it, and the meeting itself changes them.

To be open to such a transmission, one must cultivate stillness. Not the stillness of avoidance or withdrawal, but the stillness that comes from undistracted presence. The mind must be allowed to settle, the body to release habitual tension, the heart to unclench from fear or desire. Only then can the invisible teaching slip through without obstruction.

This form of instruction is not learned in the conventional sense. It cannot be captured in notes, summarized, or memorized. It is not a doctrine, not a formula, not a ritual. It is a living truth that unfolds when the student is ready to perceive it. It does not ask permission. It does not wait for readiness in the terms of the ego. But it does reveal itself fully only to those willing to let go of preconceptions, expectations, and the habitual clinging to self-identity.

The transmission is intimate. It is not broadcast widely. It is carried in subtle gestures, in the calm radiance of attention, in the unspoken alignment of being. One may be in the presence of such a teacher for years, yet if the heart and mind are not open, the teaching may pass without recognition. And yet, once recognized, it transforms instantly, bypassing the analytical mind entirely, planting its seed directly into the core of the student's awareness.

Because it requires no tongue, it communicates without deception. Words are always filtered, interpreted, and limited by language. This transmission transcends that boundary. It does not distort reality. It does not simplify. It does not embellish. It delivers the essence directly, intact, complete, and uncompromised. You feel it resonate in your being, and that resonance carries authority without assertion, clarity without explanation.

This is the language of the unspoken. A glance, a touch, a shared silence, a sustained presence. Each of these can carry more instruction than pages of writing. Each can ignite recognition, awaken memory, and reveal dimensions of understanding that would remain hidden through conventional methods. It is subtle, yet undeniable. It bypasses resistance, avoids argument, and eludes the traps of pride or defiance.

Those who are taught in this way often notice a subtle shift. They cannot describe it fully. They do not know how to integrate it through thought alone. And yet, their perception of reality changes. Their attention deepens. Their responsiveness transforms. They act with more precision, feel with more clarity, and navigate life with a new ease. The learning is embodied before it is conceptualized.

It is not uncommon for the receiver to mistake the teaching for intuition, instinct, or insight. In truth, it is all of these and more. It is a transmission that moves through the layers of consciousness, bypassing learned filters, touching what is essential and true. And because it requires no tongue, it leaves no attachment to authority. There is no hierarchy in its reception. It is pure, immediate, and unclaimed.

Once this transmission touches the core of your being, its effects ripple outward. You begin to notice the world differently. Situations that once triggered tension no longer hold the same grip. Interactions with others carry a subtle depth of understanding that requires no explanation. You respond, not react, and the clarity of action seems to emerge from a space beyond the familiar boundaries of thought.

The transmission teaches you that the source of true knowing does not reside in accumulation. It does not depend on memorization or repetition. It exists already, present and waiting. The process is not about adding to yourself but about subtracting layers of distraction and distortion until what is essential is revealed. In this space, you recognize that the teacher, the student, and the learning are all facets of a single unfolding, and distinctions begin to dissolve.

The energy of the unspoken teaching moves without effort. It does not impose itself, yet it is persistent. It carries a weight that is felt rather than seen, a gravity that aligns perception without command. Your awareness is subtly reoriented. You notice patterns in yourself that were previously invisible. You sense the motives behind habitual reactions. You understand the subtleties in the dynamics around you, not through analysis, but through direct resonance. It is an intelligence that operates beyond reasoning, yet is profoundly precise.

One of the most profound effects of this transmission is the quiet expansion it creates. It enlarges your capacity to perceive without judgment. It cultivates a patience that does not wait, a presence that is complete yet open. You no longer need to control outcomes because your attention is anchored in the truth of what is. In this state, guidance emerges naturally. Actions align effortlessly with necessity and timing. Decisions are informed not by fear or desire but by the steady wisdom that arises in the absence of noise.

This way of learning redefines authority. There is no dependence on charisma, status, or persuasion. Influence emerges from the authenticity of presence, from the coherence of being. Others may sense it without naming it. There is no pressure, no expectation, no demand for recognition. The teaching spreads because it resonates, not because it is enforced. Those who receive it are drawn into its depth through resonance alone, not through obligation or instruction.

It is also a teaching of trust. Trust in the subtle guidance that arises, trust in the readiness of the student, trust in the unfolding itself. There is no timetable, no curriculum, no syllabus. The learning is synchronous with the moment. Its rhythm cannot be anticipated or manipulated. And yet, for those who are receptive, the process feels inevitable, as if the truth was always moving toward them, never separate, never external.

Because the transmission bypasses the verbal mind, it cannot be critiqued in the usual way. Doubt arises, yet doubt itself is gently absorbed, not resisted. The teaching does not defend itself; it simply exists. Recognition comes quietly, often long after the moment of contact, when insight surfaces in action, in decision, in the clarity of perception. You understand without explanation, embody without pretense, and act without striving.

Ultimately, the unspoken transmission reveals the simplicity that underlies complexity. It shows that what you have sought externally has always been accessible internally. It invites surrender not to doctrine or personality but to the direct experience of awareness. It demonstrates that knowledge is not something to be grasped but something to be remembered, remembered in the body, in the heart, and in the unshakable stillness of consciousness.

This is the power of teaching without words. It is immediate, intimate, and transformative. It carries a depth that the loudest sermons cannot reach, a clarity that the most rigorous study cannot convey, and a presence that the mind alone cannot contain. It is the transmission that requires no tongue, yet speaks to everything.

# Chapter XIV: The Word That Was Never Written

## When Knowing Replaces Seeking

*There comes a point on the spiritual path when the inner hunger to seek begins to dissolve. Not because one has given up, but because something deeper has been found. This shift is not dramatic. It often arrives in silence, like the way dawn enters a dark room. What had once been a restless search through books, teachings, and techniques slowly quiets, not from boredom or fatigue, but from a subtle, unmistakable recognition: what I was seeking has always been here.*

---

To seek is to move from a place of perceived lack. The seeker believes something essential is missing and must be found. This impulse is not wrong. In fact, it plays a necessary role. It initiates movement. It awakens curiosity. It draws one out of the slumber of ordinary life into the deeper waters of the unseen. But like all stages, seeking is not the destination. It is a vehicle meant to be left behind once it has brought you to the threshold. When knowing arises, it does not declare itself with force. It does not need to. It is calm, grounded, and without urgency. It is not an accumulation of facts or memorized insights. It is not a belief that feels true. It is a direct experience of reality as it is, stripped of mental commentary. In knowing, you no longer reach. You no longer ask what it all means. You no longer look for someone to confirm what you feel. There is simply what is, and you are within it.

This kind of knowing cannot be produced through effort. It is not the reward of intense study or the fruit of spiritual ambition. It arrives when the inner noise has quieted enough for truth to reveal itself. And when it does, it often feels surprisingly ordinary. Not spectacular. Not dazzling. But so clear and still that it leaves no room for doubt.

In this clarity, the spiritual marketplace begins to lose its grip. You stop looking for the next retreat, the next method, the next teacher to complete you. Not out of cynicism, but because you finally see through the game.

You see that the very impulse to chase keeps you from arriving. That the search, when endlessly sustained, becomes a kind of escape. A distraction from the quiet presence that has always waited for your return.

When knowing replaces seeking, you no longer identify as someone on a journey to become something else. You are no longer trying to earn your way into wisdom. You are no longer climbing an invisible ladder toward enlightenment. You are simply aware, awake, and fully within what is here. And that here contains everything you once believed was far away.

This does not mean the path ends. What changes is your relationship to it. The need to get somewhere drops away. The tension in the body softens. The questioning mind grows quiet. And from that space, real integration begins. You no longer practice to become, but to honor what already is. Your rituals, your silence, your prayer, your stillness—none of them are tools of attainment. They become expressions of intimacy with the truth you have already tasted.

This is not the death of growth, but its flowering. And it cannot be forced. Just as a flame cannot be grabbed, this kind of knowing cannot be seized by effort. It unfolds. It opens in the absence of strain. And when it does, everything becomes different without changing at all.

You begin to see that much of what you once called "progress" was only movement in circles. Chasing an idea of awakening created by others, you mistook effort for depth and complexity for wisdom. But when the veil lifts, the real becomes simple. Not simplistic, but stripped of the decorations added by the hungry mind. The sacred reveals itself not as a destination but as presence, not as a mystery to be solved but as the unspeakable truth already living in your breath.

The mind, long conditioned to strive and label, struggles at first with this stillness. It wants to earn, to improve, to prove. It wants to compare. But the deeper knowing has no interest in competition. It does not care how far along you are. It does not rank or measure. It only asks for your willingness to be fully with what is here, without reaching toward what is not. In this, the real authority of your path is reclaimed. You stop outsourcing truth to others. You stop needing validation for your insights. You stop fearing contradiction. You know, and that is enough.

This is also where humility is reborn. Not the performance of modesty, but the kind that arises when you realize how little can be said. The more deeply you see, the less you feel the need to explain. The more intimately you know, the less you speak of it. Not because you are hiding anything, but because you understand that true knowing is not something to be displayed. It moves quietly. It lives in the background of your gestures, your presence, your gaze.

Those who reach this space often find themselves drawn more to nature than to philosophy. More to silence than to discussion. They become uninterested in defending their path or converting others. They are no longer trying to construct meaning, because they live in the pulse of what is meaningful. They don't chase miracles. They become transparent to the miraculous.

This transparency is not passive. It is not the detachment of someone who no longer cares. It is the openness of someone who no longer needs to hold on. The one who knows has no need to cling to knowing. They do not wrap it in identity or language. They wear it lightly, like something that cannot be possessed. This is why real teachers often say little. Their teaching is not in what they explain, but in what they embody. Their presence speaks what words never could.

In this space, desire becomes clean. No longer twisted by fear or insecurity, your intentions align with what is. You no longer seek to manipulate reality for gain. Instead, your actions arise from coherence with truth. Even your choices feel different. They carry no weight of future. You act, not to become, but to express. You move, not to escape, but to reflect what you are.

And yet, nothing is finished. This is not a conclusion. It is the end of illusion and the beginning of true life. Knowing is not a final state but a rhythm. It deepens. It shifts. It breathes. And it asks only one thing of you: that you stay in fidelity with what is real, no matter how subtle or confronting.

There is no certificate to mark this moment. No ceremony to announce that you have crossed into it. The world will continue as before. The noise will still rise. The mind may still doubt. But something in you no longer moves. Something in you no longer looks outward to find what you already carry.

This is the sacred rest that seekers long for without knowing it. Not the rest of inaction, but of rootedness. Not the end of growth, but the end of grasping. Here, the path continues, not from hunger, but from fullness. You no longer seek to become the light. You move as one who has seen that you were never apart from it.

# The End That Reveals the Beginning

*The journey was never linear. It only seemed that way when you believed in the distance between yourself and the truth. Each step, each turn, each trial appeared to lead you forward. You spoke of progress, awakening, expansion. You framed your path in terms of movement, as if wisdom were a destination, and not an unveiling of what had always been.*

*But there comes a moment—quiet, unassuming—when the illusion of forward motion collapses. Not because you failed, but because you arrived in the one place you were never truly apart from. It does not feel like triumph. It feels like something simpler than all your grand ideas. It feels like coming home without having known you were lost.*

---

This is the paradox at the heart of the inner journey: the end is not the conclusion. It is the unraveling of the idea that there was ever a path to walk. What once felt like striving now reveals itself as remembrance. What once felt like learning now dissolves into recognition. You return to the center not as a seeker, but as one who remembers they never left.

You may recall the early days of your path—the hunger, the fire, the ache for something more. You devoured teachings. You questioned everything. You reached for visions and revelations. You studied the maps drawn by others, hoping to find the coordinates of transcendence. There was beauty in that search, and pain too. But most of all, there was innocence. You thought the truth was far away. You thought it was hidden, reserved for the worthy or the initiated.

Now you see: what was hidden was not the truth, but your own seeing. What was distant was not the real, but your willingness to rest in it. You had built towers of thought to reach the divine, only to discover it had always been within. You circled symbols, rituals, and names, not realizing that what they pointed to had never needed language at all.

This is not a dismissal of the journey. Every step mattered. Every detour carried medicine. The failures, the disillusionments, the moments you thought you had lost your way—they carved space within you. They thinned the ego's grip. They softened the arrogance of thinking you could construct your way to the Absolute. They taught you to listen to what cannot be taught.

And now, the silence you once feared no longer feels empty. It holds you. It nourishes you. It does not need to speak, because you have begun to hear without ears. You have begun to feel without grasping. You have begun to know without naming. And in this state, time itself loses its weight. Past, present, and future fold into one another, not in theory, but in your direct experience. There is no longer a "before awakening" and "after awakening." There is only this, unfolding always, without beginning or end.

To see this is to be undone gently. It is not the kind of undoing that breaks, but the kind that releases. The kind that peels away the final layer of ambition, the final idea that something must still be achieved. You don't stop growing. But the growth is no longer for arrival. It is an expression, not a chase.

This shift is subtle but total. It changes the texture of your days. Your prayers change. Your posture in the world changes. But not in dramatic ways. You might look the same to others. You might still rise at dawn, speak with friends, plant seeds, read books. Yet everything has changed. You no longer need those things to bring you closer to something. You do them from the stillness of already-being.

You become aware that presence no longer comes and goes. It is not something you have to enter into. It is what remains when effort ceases. The old desire to return to "high states" or "pure frequencies" becomes irrelevant. You no longer confuse altered states with realization. You are not chasing light anymore. You are resting in what holds both light and shadow. The teachings you once clung to fall away, not because they were false, but because you have digested them. What once stood as scaffolding now becomes part of your structure. You do not need to recite them. They breathe through your being. You can speak truth, or remain silent, and both will carry the same resonance. Words are no longer used to reach anyone. They are simply the overflow of clarity.

In this space, paradox becomes nourishment. You no longer need to resolve it. You are both empty and full. You are both still and unfolding. You feel both the vastness of what cannot be named and the intimacy of your own breath. You do not need to explain how this can be. You simply live it.

Others may still look for signs that you have arrived—certificates, followers, language, mastery. But you are no longer seduced by the performance of wisdom. You do not need to prove your awakening. You no longer need the world to reflect it back to you. And so, strangely, the outer world may no longer hold the weight it once did. Or perhaps, it becomes even more precious, but in a quieter way. You walk through it gently, without needing to conquer or transcend it.

This is what it means to end without departure. You are here, completely. Nothing has been added to you. Nothing removed. The illusion was always the search itself. The belief that what you are was somewhere else. But the game has served its purpose. The mirror was needed only until you could see through it.

And now the beginning reveals itself again, not as something lost in time, but as something untouched. The child you were before conditioning, before striving, before performance, is not behind you. That essence is still alive, but now it walks with the knowing you've gathered. Not innocence alone, not experience alone, but the two braided together in quiet power.

This is not a peak moment. It is not a spiritual high. It does not glitter. It does not impress. But it is immovable. And because it is immovable, it is free. You can go anywhere, become anything, and still not lose it. You can speak with kings or sit alone in a cave. You can create or rest, engage or withdraw, and the center holds. The axis does not shift.

You become more available, not because you have become better, but because you are less entangled. Life moves through you with less resistance. You can act, but your actions are no longer bound by need. You can love, but your love does not grasp. You can witness the suffering of the world and serve it, but you no longer mistake yourself for the savior.

The end that reveals the beginning strips you of the illusion of becoming. What remains is not a self polished to perfection, but the mystery itself made conscious. There is no longer the question "Who am I becoming?" but only the still awareness that watches even that question dissolve.

You may smile at the old stories. You may bow to the path that brought you here. But you no longer mistake the path for the destination. You no longer mistake the teacher for the truth, or the form for the essence. You have passed through the gates not to find more answers, but to rest where questions are no longer needed.

And yet, from this place, you may begin again. Not from lack, not from seeking, but from fullness. The great circle turns. The spiral deepens. The beginning is not behind you. It lives quietly within the end. And now, you walk not to arrive, but to express the one who has always been here.

www.ingramcontent.com/pod-product-compliance
Lightning Source LLC
Chambersburg PA
CBHW050809160426
43192CB00010B/1697